MYSTERIES *of* MARTHA'S VINEYARD

Carol of the Ship's Bells

DeANNA JULIE DODSON

Mysteries of Martha's Vineyard is a trademark of Guideposts.

Published by Guideposts Books & Inspirational Media
100 Reserve Road, Suite E200
Danbury, CT 06810
Guideposts.org

Cover and interior design by Müllerhaus
Cover illustration by W Design Group, LLC.
Typeset by Aptara, Inc.

This book was previously published under the name *Water Flows Uphill* as part of the Mysteries of Martha's Vineyard series.

ISBN 978-1-961125-70-4 (hardcover)
ISBN 978-1-961125-71-1 (epub)

Printed and bound in the United States of America
10 9 8 7 6 5 4 3 2 1

Carol of the Ship's Bells

And all the bells on earth shall ring,
  On Christmas day, on Christmas day,
And all the bells on earth shall ring,
  On Christmas day in the morning.

—Traditional English Christmas Carol

CHAPTER ONE

Well, this should be interesting."

Priscilla Grant looked in the frosted front window of Rayne Forster's Gallery and Studio. The display there was a fascinating array of sculptures and paintings with a variety of styles and themes, most of them a thought-provoking mixture of traditional and modern. There was a plaster bust of Shakespeare decorated with African tribal tattoos and sporting dreadlocks sitting beside one of Genghis Khan painted bridal white wearing a beribboned wreath of pink roses and baby's breath. Next to Genghis was a trio of plaster raccoons, one lime green, one neon yellow, and one electric blue. Beside them was an amazing painting of a wooden wall with graffiti carved into it. It looked so real, so much like actual carved wood with worn blue paint flaking and peeling off, Priscilla wanted to run her fingers over it to convince herself it wasn't.

"Isn't that amazing?" her cousin Joan said, her dark eyes bright as she admired the painting. "I don't know how she makes it look so three-dimensional."

"I'm a little surprised there's nothing holiday related in there since it's Christmastime." Priscilla grinned at the foot-high skeleton in traditional South American garb standing in the corner of the display. "She certainly has eclectic taste."

"Right? I never know what's going to be in here when I pass by."

"I didn't know you liked this sort of thing," Priscilla said. "I haven't seen any at your house."

Joan shrugged. "I don't know if it's my style to actually decorate with, but it's interesting to look at, don't you think?"

"Then we should look."

Glad to get out of the December wind, Priscilla opened the door, and they both went inside. The gallery was warm and smelled of paint and sawdust and was lined with shelves filled with more of Rayne's art pieces. Some were colorful, some muted, some traditional, some modern, but most often they were a mix of at least two styles.

"I like to keep people guessing," said a melodious voice behind them.

Priscilla turned with a smile. "Are you the artist?"

The woman held out her hand, smiling too. "I'm Rayne Forster. Is there something I can show you?"

She was almost as tall as Priscilla but as slim and long limbed as a dancer. Her tanned skin was unlined except for the indications of frequent laughter around her eyes. If it weren't for the dramatic streak of white in the dark halo of her loose curls, she might have passed for twenty-five or so. As it was, Priscilla guessed she was nearer to forty. Her lavish dangling earrings and the colorful scarf she wore in a band across her hair gave her a festive look.

"We're just looking," Priscilla said, shaking her hand. It was a strong but delicate hand, the hand of an artist. "I'm Priscilla Grant.

I inherited the Misty Harbor lighthouse along with the cottage when my aunt died, so I moved here from Kansas."

"Oh," Rayne said. "So that's you. I hear you have a museum in the lighthouse too. I really need to come see it. I'm thinking of doing some seascapes, and that lighthouse might just inspire me."

"I'd love to show you around," Priscilla said, and she gave her a card. "Call me when you have time to come by."

"I'll do that." Rayne smiled at Joan. "And you've been in here before."

"This is my cousin, Joan Abernathy," Priscilla said.

Rayne shook Joan's hand too. "I'm sorry I didn't get to introduce myself one of those other times."

"You were busy with customers when I was here before," Joan told her. "I didn't want to interrupt. But my cousin and I were going by, and I just had to show her some of your things. They're so unique."

Rayne shrugged, looking faintly pleased. "As I said, I like to keep people guessing."

They stopped to view a clay sculpture of a woman's head. It had been very convincingly painted to appear as if it was actually formed out of wire mesh that you could look through to see a Parisian sidewalk café. But the café windows were cracked and broken, the awning hung in tattered strips from its frame, one of the metal chairs was turned on its side, and bits of newspaper and other debris lay on the sidewalk, the romantic scene neglected and abandoned. Priscilla was about to ask about the meaning behind it when the door opened and a man came into the gallery. He was a little stocky and in his midfifties, Priscilla thought, but he was a natty dresser. When he spotted Joan, he turned on a smile that was certainly engaging.

"Well, hello." He swept the fedora off his head. "I didn't expect to see you in here again."

Joan's cheeks turned pinker than the winter wind had already made them. "Hello, Calvin. I didn't think you'd be back yet."

"I got to Lima in record time and found that my native craftsman has been working overtime." He winked at Rayne. "Do you have room for another shipment, honey? I think these new ones are going to sell like hotcakes."

Rayne laughed and shook her head. "I don't know how you always know what's popular, but I'll never argue with success."

"I told you everything would be snapped up in a day or two." The man grinned. "You be the artist, I'll take care of the imports, okay?"

She shrugged. "I'm just selling what you bring in. What you decide to ship over here is your own business."

"Nice and simple, just like I like it." He turned again to Joan. "So, what have you been up to since I left? Who's your friend?"

"My cousin, Priscilla Grant. Priscilla, this is Calvin Gallico. He imports artwork from all over the world."

"You two have met before, I see," Priscilla said.

Joan nodded. "When I was in here about a month ago. Calvin was talking to Rayne about selling some of his imports from her gallery, and I was coming in as he was going out. Then a couple of weeks ago, we ran into each other again and started talking."

The man beamed at Joan. "You don't know how hard it is to find someone who can carry on a good conversation anymore, Priscilla. And to find out Joan here is an artist herself, well, it was just a pleasure to talk to her."

"Now, Calvin," Joan said, the pink in her cheeks deepening. "You know I'm just an amateur."

"An artist!" Rayne said. "What sort of things do you do?"

"Oh, it's not much. Not real art like yours."

Rayne chuckled. "I don't know about that. I guess some of my stuff is 'real art.' A lot of it is just fun. That's the stuff that seems to sell anyhow. People like my mash-ups."

"But you're a working artist," Joan told her. "I just do a few still lifes. Only for fun."

"You sold a couple," Priscilla reminded her.

Calvin's eyes lit. "You never told me that. That's great. I bet I could find some collectors who'd be interested in some of your work too."

"Stop," Joan said with a shy grin, and she pushed a lock of short brown hair behind her ear.

Calvin gave her an exaggerated wink, and that made her laugh. Was he flirting? And was she flirting back?

"So you're an importer?" Priscilla asked the man.

One hand over his heart, he made a slight bow. "I am. I deal in volume more than high price. Mostly little things anyone can afford, things folks can pick up on a whim and not worry about paying for. Interesting little things from all over. A lot of them handcrafted. I'll tell you what, honey, all those little nickels and dimes certainly add up after a while. I just have to keep finding artists who can keep up with the demand."

"Have you decided what you're going to bring in next?" Rayne asked.

Calvin nodded eagerly. "This guy I met is going to make more of the same kind of pottery I brought this time but bigger. Really impressive, you know? I think they'll sell well. In fact, I know several collectors who'll be really interested. Still want to carry them here? Same terms?"

"That will be great."

They shook hands on it, and then Calvin turned back to Joan.

"I have to meet a guy, but uh, I was wondering if you might want to have coffee or something. Maybe in the morning? And I heard the pond's frozen over. What would you say to going ice-skating sometime?"

Joan laughed. "Me? I haven't been skating in years."

"Me either," he said, his eyes twinkling, "so what could we lose?"

Joan laughed again, and then they both glanced at Priscilla.

"While they're making plans," Priscilla said to Rayne, feeling terribly in the way, "would you mind telling me about this sculpture? Is the woman dreaming of Paris? And what happened to her?"

"I hate to interpret anything for viewers," the artist said, walking with Priscilla toward the piece. "I think each person brings his or her own meaning to any creative work."

As she spoke about the variety of reactions her creations evoked, Priscilla couldn't help glancing over at her cousin. Joan and Calvin were chatting away about who knew what, neither of them seeming to notice that Priscilla and Rayne were on the other side of the room now.

After she and Rayne talked a moment more about the sculpture and Rayne's art in general, Priscilla took another look back at Joan.

"What's this about ice-skating? I always thought it was too warm here in December for anything but slush most of the time."

"Evidently not this year," Rayne said. "It's been cold enough for a long enough spell to make a good sheet of ice. I'm told it doesn't happen often, so it's kind of a treat when it does. Do you skate?"

"Not really. I do have some skates. I think. My husband and I went a few times years ago when one of the malls put in a rink. I'm not even sure if I brought them with me up here." Priscilla glanced at Joan and her friend and lowered her voice. "Have you known him long?"

Rayne shrugged. "A few weeks now. I don't know how much he really knows about art, but he evidently knows what sells. And I never turn down anything that brings in a paying customer."

"Do you know much about him?"

"Not really," Rayne admitted. "I know he's got a boat of some kind that he takes all over so he can pick up things to sell to collectors here. That's about it."

"Interesting." *Odd* was what Priscilla was really thinking, but she didn't say that aloud. Instead she smiled over at Joan. "Are we still going to the library?"

"Sure." Joan turned to Calvin. "It was good to run into you again. I'd love to hear about your last trip."

"Tomorrow at eight," he said. "Now don't you forget."

"I won't."

He nodded at Priscilla and Rayne. "Good to meet you, Priscilla. I'll be in touch, Rayne." He replaced his hat and turned up the collar on his coat. "Oh, I'll bring the new stuff over some-time tomorrow if it's all right."

"Just fine," Rayne said. "Anytime after lunch."

"Till tomorrow," Calvin said to Joan, "and Merry Christmas, everybody." He stuffed his hands into his pockets and hurried into the street.

"What's this about tomorrow at eight?" Priscilla asked, making her expression very arch.

"Just coffee." Joan colored again and looked around the studio. "I do want to go to the library, but I haven't gotten around to looking at everything here yet."

"There are a lot of things to see." Priscilla gave her arm a squeeze, smiling. "And I hope you have a nice time with Calvin tomorrow."

Rayne was good enough to show them around the gallery and then give them a look at her studio. The former was artistically laid out, showing each piece to advantage. The latter could only be described as controlled chaos.

"I never know what I'm going to want to do next," Rayne said with a sheepish grin.

The large table in the center of the room was filled with her works in progress and covered with bits and pieces of just about everything imaginable. Around it was shelves full of supplies: paints and plaster mixes, various tools and brushes, and dozens of molds, classic and modern, austere and whimsical. Most interesting were the bins of what Rayne called "found stuff."

"Not that I found it at the dump," she explained, "not most of it anyway, but I did find it here and there, at thrift stores and antique stores and craft shops. Even office supply stores and beauty shops and a grocery store or two. I never know what I might need until I get started."

"Unless you have a commission, right?" Priscilla asked.

"Right."

"What kinds of things does Calvin usually bring in?" Joan asked.

"Oh, it depends on where he's been." Rayne walked them over to one of the shelves where there were several colorful items that looked like they were from South America. "A lot of earthenware lately. These handmade dolls have been very popular. I sold out of the alpaca-wool blankets he got on his last trip. It's always interesting to see what he comes up with."

"It must be," Priscilla said.

Rayne shrugged good-naturedly. "I'm just glad he knows better than I do what will sell. Of course, I'd rather sell my own stuff, but this helps pay the bills."

"You never know when you'll hit it big," Joan said. "Or when your luck will change." She glanced toward the front door.

"Thanks for showing us around, Rayne," Priscilla said. "It was nice meeting you. Good luck with your imports."

"Thanks." Rayne showed them to the door. "Come back anytime, and stay warm."

Priscilla buttoned her coat at the collar and pulled on the knitted cap she had in her pocket, and then she and Joan went back out into the cold. They made small talk on the walk back to the car and the short drive to the library. Once there, they returned the books they had checked out, chatted for a moment with Clara, the head librarian, and then checked out the books she had been holding for them.

"What do you think about stopping at Candy's for some coffee?" Priscilla asked once they were back in the car.

Joan looked exaggeratedly thoughtful. "I don't know. Will cookies be involved?"

"They could be."

"Then I think we should absolutely stop by."

For Christmas, Candy Lane Confectionery was all glitzed up to look like a candy shop at the North Pole, and Priscilla couldn't help smiling at the little elf dolls that were peeping out of every available space. The shop was never very busy on a Tuesday afternoon during the winter, and she wasn't surprised to find most of the café-style tables available. She and Joan ordered coffee and chocolate-chip cookies at the counter and then seated themselves at one of the tables near the window.

"Looking for something?" Priscilla asked playfully when Joan sat staring out over the harbor and the winter-gray sea beyond, obviously not hearing anything Priscilla had been saying.

"Sorry." Joan laughed half under her breath. "Just looking." After one more quick glance, she turned back to Priscilla. "How's Jake these days?"

Joan saw Priscilla's dog, Jake, all the time.

"Same as when you saw him on Sunday. How's Sister?"

Sister was the puppy Priscilla had given Joan last spring. Priscilla saw her all the time too.

"A bundle of energy as always," Joan said with a wry grin, "but I guess you knew that already too."

"So tell me what's really on your mind. Is it—"

Priscilla broke off as the girl behind the counter brought their coffee and cookies and left the check. Joan made a great show of putting sugar and cream in her coffee and then stirring it.

"Is it that man who was in the gallery?" Priscilla asked finally. "Calvin?"

"Is what him?"

"Is he what's on your mind?"

Joan shrugged. "Maybe. A little. I was just wondering if I might see his boat out there."

"So he really picks up all his imports himself? That seems a little bit...inefficient."

"Well, I don't think he does all of it. He just gathers up different things he thinks his buyers over here would like and then, if they're interested in particular ones, he gets the artists to make up a lot of them to be shipped over. But he shows buyers the samples and takes their orders."

"Sounds like you and he have had time to talk," Priscilla said.

Joan bit her lip. "You don't like him."

"Hey, I didn't say that. I've hardly met him." Priscilla reached over and patted her cousin's hand. "I'm not trying to grill you or anything. I'm just curious, and you seemed a little bit distracted. You don't have to tell me about him if you don't want to."

"No, it's nothing like that. I just don't have that much to tell. We met at the gallery, and we talked for a while. Then I saw him downtown one day, and we decided to have a sandwich at the Nautilus Café. It was nice. He's been a lot of interesting places, and we just talked."

"What did you say his last name is?" Priscilla asked.

"Gallico. Calvin Gallico. He lives in Boston, but he's always looking for artists who can make things he can import. With all the trips he makes, he says he's almost never home."

"No family then."

"Not really. No kids." Joan looked thoughtful. "He was married for seventeen years, but then she died and he hasn't met anyone since then. Sort of like me losing Allan."

"At least you have your boys."

Joan pressed her lips together. "That's not exactly a substitute, is it."

Priscilla could have bitten her tongue. Being a widow herself, she knew it wasn't. Motherhood was about preparing a child for a future and independence, for setting out into a separate life. Marriage was molding two separate lives into one. As much as she loved her daughter, Rachel, being a mother was no substitute for being a wife, for being a partner and a helpmate and a lover. It was no substitute at all.

"Sorry. That didn't exactly come out the way I meant it to."

"No, I'm sorry." Joan winced. "I didn't mean to snap at you. Anyway, I just had a sandwich with the guy. It's not like we signed a prenuptial agreement."

"Well, I think it would be nice if you met someone you liked. It just seems like it would be a hassle if he didn't even live on the island and was gone all the time."

"I don't know. I've gotten pretty set in my ways since Allan died. I may not be ready to have someone around all the time again. But it won't hurt to have a cup of coffee with him, right?"

"Or go ice-skating?" Priscilla teased.

"We don't have any definite plans for that. Yet."

"Keep your eyes open anyway," Priscilla said. "At least until you know more about him. Maybe he still has a wife in Boston."

Joan rolled her eyes.

"And another one in Brazil," Priscilla added with a grin.

"He was in Peru," Joan said primly. "Drink your coffee."

CHAPTER TWO

Delicious," Gerald O'Bannon said two nights later, pushing his plate away. "Delicious as always."

Priscilla and Gerald often had dinner together. Tonight, he had come to Priscilla's cottage straight from the Coast Guard station, so he still wore the short-sleeved shirt and navy-blue pants of his captain's uniform. His hat dangled from the back of his chair. Priscilla couldn't help smiling at the way he always seemed to have a wavy lock of hair fallen over his forehead.

"It was just roasted potatoes and chicken," she told him, but it pleased her very much to know he liked her cooking.

"But it's *your* roasted potatoes and chicken." He reached across the table to squeeze her fingers. "And that makes all the difference."

"Flatterer," she said, though she had made those potatoes, her mother's special recipe with broccoli and bacon, especially for him. "But flattery will get you Lane Cake."

His eyes lit. "My favorite. I'll take that trade any time of the year."

She got up and started clearing the table. "Do you want it now or later on?"

"In a little while." He got up too and began gathering dishes. "But only if you let me clear up and help you load the dishwasher."

"I never say no to some help."

"You got it."

He followed her into the kitchen, arms loaded. While she put the leftovers into storage containers, he began rinsing food off the dishes and the baking pans.

"So how's your week been?" he asked, raising his voice over the tinny spray of water against the chicken pan. "We haven't had a chance to catch up since church."

"Mostly just the same old thing," she told him. "Did some work on the museum."

"Yeah?"

"Maybe you could help me with a display about the Coast Guard and its connection to the lighthouse since it was built."

"That sounds good. We could definitely figure out something." He turned the pan over, gave it another good scrub, and then rinsed it and set it on the drying rack. "I hear Uncle Seth's Pond is frozen now."

"That's what I hear too. I didn't know it was such a big deal on the island."

"Maybe not a huge deal, but it's unusual enough to get people excited. It's like a Christmas treat. We should go sometime. What do you think?"

"I'm not sure how good I'd be at it. I've been only a few times and that was years ago, but it was a lot of fun."

"You think about it," he said, taking another dish from the sink. "But don't wait too long. Weather like this may not last."

She couldn't help smiling at the bright eagerness in his eyes. "I'll see if I can find my old skates. If I can, we'll do it."

"Great."

They worked through more of the dishes in companionable silence.

"I saw Joan at the dog park yesterday with Sister," Gerald said as he wiped the last of the platters. "That's one cute little pup."

"Isn't she?" Priscilla handed him the now-empty bowl she had served the potatoes in. "And she's getting so big. How did she and Sammy get along?"

She was very fond of Gerald's dog, a sweet-tempered female Irish setter who was getting up in years.

"Oh, we didn't stop," Gerald explained as he rinsed out the bowl. "Sam wanted to go play with Sister like she usually does when we see her in the park, but Joan was talking to someone, and we didn't want to interrupt."

"Someone?"

Gerald shrugged. "Some guy. I don't know."

Priscilla shut the refrigerator door and brought the rest of the empty serving dishes to the sink. "A guy about fifty-something? Not so tall? A little heavy? Maybe wearing a hat?"

"Yeah, that might be him. Do you know him?"

"I've met him." She started loading the dishwasher. "Joan and I went into that art gallery downtown on Tuesday."

"Art Attack?"

"No, the newer one. Well, not brand new. Rayne's."

"Oh, yeah." Gerald grinned a little. "She's got an interesting style."

"I think so. She seems really nice too. Anyway, the guy came in when Joan and I were there. She said she's met him a couple of times."

Gerald looked at her expectantly. "And?"

"Well, nothing really. They were going to have coffee the next day, and I guess he went with her to the dog park."

Gerald handed her a wet plate. "Sounds pleasant enough. You don't have any objections, do you?"

"Not really." She put the plate in the dishwasher rack, considering. "I think it would be great if Joan found someone. She's been alone for too long."

"But?"

"But what? I didn't say 'but' anything."

"You might as well have." Gerald handed her another plate. "Don't you like him?"

"I guess I do. I mean, I don't know him at all. He's an importer. He was in talking to Rayne about some pottery he wants to sell in her gallery."

"What's wrong with that?"

She shook her head. "Nothing. Really, nothing at all. He just seemed to come on a little strong, that's all. Like a used-car salesman."

Gerald handed her the last plate and started on the silverware. "Somebody's got to sell 'em."

Priscilla laughed in spite of herself. "I know. And Rayne seemed happy enough to work with him. He buys things from artists in various countries and then brings them to Rayne to sell, on consignment, I guess, so she doesn't actually risk anything."

"Nothing shady about that."

"Now, I'm not saying he's shady." She put the rest of the dishes into the dishwasher and then started helping him rinse the silverware. "I just don't know about him. I love Joan with all my heart, and I don't want anybody taking advantage of her. He just seems too slick. Too much too soon."

"I don't know," Gerald said. "You never know what makes a couple click. Joan's a nice lady. Who wouldn't like her?"

"I'm not saying a man might not like her. I'm sure the right one would love her dearly and be lucky to have her, but not after saying hello a couple of times in an art gallery and then going to have a sandwich and coffee."

Gerald frowned and turned off the water. "Are you telling me he's asked her to marry him or something?"

"No, no, nothing like that." She handed him a towel to dry his hands. "But he does seem awfully interested. Though I guess she is too. Kinda."

"Maybe he's just lonely. What did you say he did? Import art from all over? If he travels all the time, he probably has a hard time keeping a relationship going for very long. Women like a guy who's around, you know?"

She smiled into his eyes. "They sure do."

"So why not see what happens?" He filled the soap dispenser, shut the dishwasher door, and turned it on. The hum of machinery and swish of water filled the kitchen. "He might be the best thing that ever happened to her."

"But what if—"

"'What if' hasn't happened yet, right?" He took her hand and tucked it into his elbow. "What if you let Joan be in control of her own life and decide who she wants to spend time with?"

She exhaled and then nodded. "You're right. I just don't want to see her hurt."

"And neither do I." He walked her into the living room where Jake was snoozing under the twinkling lights of the Christmas tree, and sat down. "So if you notice anything that seems off to you, and I mean besides him being too brash for your taste, let me know. I can have him checked out."

"That would be great. And, no, to be honest, I don't know of anything at this point. He has a boat docked somewhere, but I don't know the name or even what kind it is. Something he could take some pretty long trips in."

"What's his name?" Gerald asked, taking a little notebook and a pen from his pocket.

"Calvin Gallico. Joan says he lives in Boston."

Gerald wrote the name down. "Okay. Just for future reference. But I don't want you to worry. Joan's a big girl. She can take care of herself."

"I know. I just—"

Gerald's cell phone rang. "I'm sorry. I meant to turn that off."

"No problem," she said. "You'd better see who it is."

He checked the display and then smiled. "It's Aggie." He pressed talk. "Hey, Aggie. How's my favorite daughter?"

Priscilla couldn't hear the words, but she could clearly hear the distress in Aggie's voice. Gerald's smile vanished.

"What? How is she?" He listened for another minute and then glanced at Priscilla. "Look, honey, I'd better come over. Is that all right? Let me tell Priscilla good night, and then I'll head that way. I want you to tell me everything, okay?"

"What's wrong?" Priscilla asked when he ended the call. "Is Aggie okay? How's Ava?"

Gerald's granddaughter, Ava, was only a year old.

He raked both hands through his hair and then got to his feet. "I'm sorry, but I really have to go. Aggie just brought the baby back from having some tests done. She's got something wrong with one of the valves in her heart. Aggie says it's called aortic regurgitation. It's like a leak in the valve."

"Oh, Gerald, I'm so sorry. Is there anything I can do?"

"I really don't know any details yet," he said as he tugged on his coat, "but I'd sure appreciate you praying for her. And for all of us to be able to get through this."

"I sure will." She hugged him. "Call me if there's something I can do to help or if you just want to talk."

"Thanks." He tightened the embrace and then grabbed his hat from his chair in the kitchen and was gone.

Priscilla stared out into the blustery darkness, watching as he drove away. Then she went back to the couch and sat down. The opening and closing of the front door had wakened Jake, and now he came over to her, pressing himself against her leg, pushing his muzzle into her hand. She sighed and then threw her arms around his neck.

Poor Gerald, he must be terrified. Her own daughter was grown and on her own, but Priscilla couldn't imagine how afraid she would be if Rachel had been given such a diagnosis. How much worse must it be for Gerald when he was worried about little Ava and his daughter Aggie on top of that?

"Oh, Jake," Priscilla whispered, and then, still clinging to him, she bowed her head and started to pray.

Priscilla was getting ready for bed about three hours later when her phone rang. She answered immediately.

"Gerald?"

"Hi." His voice sounded tired. "Am I calling too late?"

"No, of course not. I've been worried about you. What did you find out?"

He exhaled. "I don't know all the technical stuff. Just a leak in the baby's heart. They usually find this kind of thing really early, but not in this case. It's kind of severe now, but the good news is that the doctor seems to think it can be fixed. He says they have a really good success rate, especially with little ones who are as healthy as Ava is otherwise."

"Oh, thank God. That's wonderful."

"Yeah, it is. I know Aggie's scared about it and so am I, but the doctor told her they do this all the time and Ava should be fine."

He didn't sound that relieved.

"What aren't you telling me?" she asked finally.

"You know how it is." He laughed humorlessly. "Aggie and Nick don't have a clue how they'll pay for all this. I told them I'd help, and I will, but who knows how much it's going to cost? Aggie hasn't even started talking to their insurance company yet, but I know they have a high deductible and all kinds of hurdles to jump before the insurance pays anything at all. She hadn't told me this before, but she and Nick have been struggling just trying to make ends meet since Ava was born. Now this on top of everything. They don't know what they're going to do."

"I guess trying to borrow more would just make a bad situation worse."

"They're like a lot of people, totally borrowed up. You know, I was glad when Aggie was able to stay home with the kids. It was something she really wanted to do."

"I'm glad she could too," Priscilla said. "I know it's not something you can take for granted anymore. It's hard for families to make it on one income these days."

Gerald sighed. "All kinds of people are in all kinds of situations and have to figure out what works best for them. I just wish Aggie and Nick hadn't gone into debt trying to keep up with the Joneses."

"A lot of people do it," Priscilla said. "And then it's really hard to get out, especially when something unexpected happens. Maybe it won't be as bad as they think. The cost, I mean."

"You're right," he said, and she could hear the smile in his voice. "No use counting on trouble that might not come."

"Are you going to be able to sleep tonight?" she asked.

"Yeah, sure. We'll figure out something, and knowing Ava's going to be okay is the most important thing. I mean, they can't give us any guarantees or anything, of course, but they say it's pretty routine and shouldn't be an issue later on. Thank God for that."

"Yes, thank God."

"The rest is just…money. We'll work it out. I just don't like Aggie and Nick to be so worried about this, the cost on top of everything else. I want to figure out something I can do to take some of that load off them."

"You're a good dad," she told him. "And a good granddad."

"And you're a good listener. Thanks for hearing me out." He drew a deep breath. "And thanks for praying. Please don't stop."

"I won't. I promise." She wished she was with him now so she could give him a hug, so she could do something to make him feel better. "And please don't ever think you can't call me or come by to talk. You're always welcome, and no apologies needed."

"Thanks. It's good to have somebody to talk to who understands."

"I do. You know I'd do anything for Rachel, and I know you'd do anything for Aggie and for Ava."

"I would," he said. "Absolutely anything."

After they said good night and Priscilla was drifting off to sleep, she remembered what he said. She had no doubt whatsoever that he would. Anything.

CHAPTER THREE

The next morning, Priscilla took Jake for a long walk. She couldn't help thinking about little Ava and her worried parents and poor Gerald. The baby and her older brother, Max, meant the world to him. Maybe there was something she could do to help too. But there wasn't much she could do besides speculate until Aggie found out more about what Ava's tests and surgery would cost and what the insurance would cover. Even then, Gerald wasn't likely to talk about it in detail. He could be very private about things like this, especially when the information in question wasn't actually his own.

Of course, she had told him about Joan and this Calvin guy, but that wasn't exactly personal information. And it wasn't exactly serious. Nothing like what Gerald was going through with his family. Still, it was something else to keep Priscilla from enjoying her morning walk.

She was cold and hungry when she and Jake got back home. He seemed disappointed that she hadn't wanted to romp with him or even talk much.

"Sorry, boy." She patted him after she filled his bowl with food and then gave him fresh water. "I guess I have a lot on my mind."

She fixed herself some eggs, toast, and coffee and then sat in the kitchen looking out the window at nothing. When she was through, she placed her dishes in the sink. Then she shook her head.

"I am not going to mope around here all day. It's a gloomy day and I've heard some gloomy news and I have gloomy feelings about this Calvin guy, but I'm not going to let that make me gloomy too." She straightened her shoulders and then shook her finger at Jake. "Do you hear that, Jake? I'm not going to be gloomy."

The dog looked at her from the corner of his eye, but evidently not finding her statement particularly relevant to his interests, he went back to his breakfast. She laughed, patted his head, then went to make herself presentable enough to be seen in public.

She had several errands to run, the last of which was a visit to the East Shore Historical Museum. The Queen Anne Victorian house where the museum was located was painted a sunny yellow, a bright spot in the winter dreariness, and she was glad when the curator, Mildred Pearson, welcomed her inside with the offer of a cup of hot coffee.

"What are you up to today?" Mildred asked once they were both seated at the little table in the museum's kitchen. She was dressed like a housewife from the late eighteenth century, her full-skirted gown a pretty cotton print, a lace shawl around her shoulders, and her gray hair piled atop her head and covered by a mobcap. She didn't look quite in place next to the refrigerator and coffee machine. "Did you hear Seth's Pond is frozen?"

Priscilla grinned. "I did, as a matter of fact. Are you going skating?"

"I just might at that." Mildred gave her a confident nod. "I have some skates from the late eighteenth century that I'd love to try. I wouldn't want to damage them by actually putting them on, but oh, it's tempting. If I do go, though, I have some of my own. I wasn't half bad last time I gave it a try."

"I didn't realize everybody would get so excited about a cold snap."

Mildred looked amused. "I guess it's a nice change from slush. Oh, thirty or forty years ago, we had skating weather all the time in the winter. Now it's only a few days a year, but that makes it special. So what brings you to the museum today?"

"I just wanted to get out of the house more than anything," Priscilla said. "I thought I'd see what kind of displays you have about the Coast Guard, if any. Gerald said he'd help me figure out something for my museum to show how the lighthouse and the Coast Guard both have helped make the coast safe for sailing vessels, and I didn't want to copy anything you already have."

"We don't have much about the Coast Guard directly. Just a mention or two here and there. I think it's high time somebody had something like that though, and the lighthouse is the perfect place for it. When we've finished our coffee, I'll show you what we have."

"Great," Priscilla said. "I'm in no hurry. How's Oreo? I mean Hiacoomes."

The black-and-white cat had been a stray that Priscilla had fed from time to time before Mildred had adopted him and renamed him for a Martha's Vineyard Native American from the 1600s. The name was an unusual one, but she had a feeling the cat didn't mind being called by it as long as he was called in time for meals.

Mildred chuckled. "He's all cat. I don't know how I ever got along without him. How's Jake?"

"He's wonderful. He puts up with me and doesn't even complain."

The bell at the museum's front door jingled. Mildred took another sip of coffee, then stood up.

"So much for our chat. I'll be back."

"No rush," Priscilla said. "I'm going to finish my coffee, and then I'll catch up with you."

She found Mildred a few minutes later showing a man one of the museum's fully accessorized rooms. He was tall and lanky, looked to be somewhere in his thirties, and wore his long sandy-blond hair in a ponytail down his back. Behind the tinted granny glasses, his gray eyes were scanning the 1812 parlor.

"As you can see," Mildred was saying, "most of what we have is Americana from the colonial period forward. We do have some North American Indian artifacts and displays, but nothing from Central or South America."

"I realize that's not very usual for this part of the country," he said. "I was just hoping you might know someone who does know about it. A collector maybe? Or a dealer?"

Mildred smiled. "I'm sorry, but I really don't. I understand it's fascinating, but it's hard enough to keep up with everything I need to know about what we have in the museum already."

Priscilla came a little closer, waiting for a lull in their conversation. The man looked at her inquiringly, and she gave him a tentative smile.

"Excuse me. I didn't mean to eavesdrop or anything. You're looking for South American art?"

He smiled back. "No problem. I'm a collector of sorts."

"Isn't Martha's Vineyard an unusual place to look for that kind of thing? Maybe New York City or even Boston would be a better place to try."

"I didn't want to deal with one of the big galleries. Sure, there are costs involved in bringing stuff into the country, and I don't mind paying for that. I don't mind an importer making a decent living, but those big places go way overboard. I'm not interested in paying for their marble floors and crystal chandeliers."

"I guess I never really thought about that before," Mildred said, "but I don't know of any of the major galleries here on the island that would carry that sort of thing, and you don't want a big gallery in the first place, right? You might try—"

"There's Rayne's," Priscilla said. "I was over at her place the other day and she was talking to an importer, and I think he was just in Peru. Rayne said he brought her several items to sell in her shop, but from the way she described them, they're probably not the kind of things a real collector would be interested in. Handmade wool blankets, little native dolls, pottery. They're authentic, but not expensive. Just a curiosity, I guess."

"Rayne's?" the man asked, his sandy eyebrows going up over the frame of his glasses.

"She's got a little gallery not far from here." Priscilla gave him directions. "She can tell you a lot more about what she has for sale right now than I can."

He finished scribbling down the information she had given him and then stuffed the paper into the pocket of his worn jeans. "Thanks. I appreciate you both talking to me."

Mildred nodded. "Is there anything else you'd like to see here, Mr....?"

"Oh, Weir. Justin Weir. I'm from New Jersey, but I do a lot of traveling, looking for...whatever interests me."

He grinned a little at that, and Priscilla wondered, just looking at him, how he managed to afford traveling around doing nothing but collecting *objets d'art*.

"Will you be on the island long?" Mildred asked, and then she stopped herself. "Excuse me, and please let me introduce myself. I'm Mildred Pearson, and this is Priscilla Grant. She owns the museum in the Misty Harbor Lighthouse."

Justin's eyes lit. "I'll have to come by and see your exhibits too. You don't happen to have any native artifacts, do you?"

Priscilla laughed. "No, I'm afraid not. Not South American anyway, though we do have a few items that the Wampanoag tribe gave my ancestors, ones that have been passed down to me and some of my relations. The museum is mostly about my family, the Lathams, and the lighthouse and the sea. I hope you'll come by anyway. You might find something interesting there."

"I'll do that. Even though the North American tribes aren't my particular interest, their history and customs are fascinating. The more you know, the more interesting it gets," Justin told her. "Thanks for your help, Mrs. Pearson. And thank you for the information about Rayne's, Mrs. Grant. I appreciate the help."

Priscilla smiled and nodded.

Mildred waited until the bell on the front door rang again before she said anything. "That may be one of the most unusual requests I've had for the museum."

"I don't quite know what to make of him," Priscilla said. "He doesn't dress like someone who's independently wealthy, but he must have some money if all he does is go around collecting stuff he's interested in."

"Maybe he's a trust-fund baby."

"Could be, I guess," Priscilla said, "but you're right. Martha's Vineyard is not the first place I'd come looking for South American art, even if he was the silk suit and buttoned-down shirt type."

"Speaking of the buttoned-down shirt type." Mildred glanced toward the door, then turned back to Priscilla. "Who is that man your cousin's been going around with?"

"Going around with?"

"Well, I don't know if they're dating, but I have seen them a time or two around town. They were in here yesterday, which is what made me think of them."

Priscilla didn't like to say anything about the situation, especially since she didn't know much. And she didn't want to say anything that might make Mildred dislike the man based on her own unfounded feelings. She found herself wanting desperately to call Gerald and ask him to check out the guy anyway, actual reasons or not, but she didn't want to do that to him. He had enough to worry about right now, and she wasn't going to dump her concerns on top of that, petty as they were. She merely shrugged.

"I just met the man, so I don't know much. Joan says they're only friends. I suppose he'll be on his way before long. Evidently, his business takes him all over the world, and when he comes back to the US he brings things to sell. Sounds to me like he doesn't usually have the opportunity to really get to know people."

"Well, Joan looked like she was having fun. I'm happy for her."

"I'd love for her to find someone," Priscilla said, and it was true. "But I don't know if there's anything to this. I guess we'll see."

"How about we look at those exhibits you were wondering about?" Mildred asked. "As I said, we don't have all that much, but you might find something helpful."

They spent another half hour looking at what the museum had about the Coast Guard, and then Priscilla went home and took Jake for a walk. She hadn't been back home more than twenty minutes when her phone rang. It was her cousin Trudy, Joan's younger sister.

"It's frozen!" Trudy said before Priscilla could even say hello. "The pond is frozen!"

"Hey, Trudy." Priscilla was used to Trudy's excitability and never let it hurry her. "I've heard that. Are you going to skate?"

"Dan and I are planning to go tomorrow night or the next." She sighed dreamily. "So romantic."

Priscilla felt a little twinge of longing at the thought, but she wouldn't allow herself to daydream about how it would be to glide across the moonlit ice at Gerald's side. They were friends, and she wasn't going to spoil that with expectations.

"So how are you?" she asked Trudy instead.

"Oh, I'm fine, but that's not important. Joan's being awfully sneaky about this man she met, and I want to know what you think of him!"

Trudy hardly ever said anything that wasn't emphatic.

"Sneaky?" Priscilla asked. "What do you mean by sneaky?"

"Oh, you know."

"You mean she didn't bring him straight over to your house so he could tell you his life story and innermost hopes and dreams?"

Trudy snickered. "Okay, maybe not sneaky exactly, but she sure isn't telling anybody about him."

"Maybe there's just nothing to tell. I saw him for just a few minutes at the Rayne Forster studio," Priscilla said, "so I can't really tell you much myself. He might be a few years younger than Joan, but not much. He seems to be well off. He imports things from all over. That's about it."

"I know all that. Candy already told us." *Us* could only mean Trudy and their mutual cousin Gail. "Of course, Gail said we ought to stay out of it and let Joan see who she wants to see."

"I'm sure she's right," Priscilla said, not the least bit surprised to hear that's what Gail had said. Gail had a not-yet-common-knowledge romance going on herself, so it stood to reason she would be sensitive about Joan being given her privacy even if this was only a potential relationship. Of course, she didn't mention that to Trudy.

"But who is he?" Trudy demanded. "What's he like?"

"I already told you everything I know."

Trudy huffed. "But what kind of impression did he give you? Did you like him?"

What to say? Priscilla didn't want to prejudice anyone against the man just because she wasn't sure about him herself, but she didn't want to say he seemed like a great guy when she didn't feel that way either.

"Really, Trudy, I don't know. He seems to like Joan a lot. I don't know if she's really interested in him or just flattered, but she did look like she was enjoying the attention. I don't guess there's any harm in that, is there? Not as long as she doesn't make any more of it than that until she knows him better."

"Oh, I guess you're right." There was a definite pout in Trudy's voice. "But that's just not very exciting either."

That made Priscilla laugh. "I know. How disappointing of Joan to not be more entertaining."

Trudy giggled. "You know what I mean. But, really, do you think it could be something serious?"

"That I just don't know. I told you I barely spoke to him. I suppose all we can do is see what happens in the future. Joan's a big girl and—"

"Yes, I know. I've already had that lecture." Trudy paused for a second. "You said you met him at the Forster studio, right? I think I'll go over there and see what she knows about him. If she's selling imports for him, she must know *something*."

Priscilla winced. They had to be careful. Joan wouldn't like it if she knew they were checking up on her.

"What if we both go talk to Rayne and ask her about her art and things like that and just casually get her to talk about Calvin?"

"Sure," Trudy said. "I can do casual."

Priscilla wasn't entirely convinced, but it was better than nothing. "All right. Are you free right now?"

"Now would be perfect."

"I'll be right over."

Trudy got into Priscilla's SUV, her blond curls hidden under a bright yellow knitted cap, her petite frame bulked up in a heavy coat, and her blue eyes wide. "I was just thinking," she said. "It's Friday afternoon. What if Rayne closes early on Fridays?"

"Then we'll go back tomorrow," Priscilla assured her as she pulled away from the curb. "And if she's not open Saturdays, we'll go back Monday. Just keep it casual. If she thinks we're up to something, she probably won't tell us anything."

On the drive over, Priscilla told her about Rayne and her shop.

"I guess I've never really paid attention," Trudy said. "I mean, I know where it is and everything, but I've never noticed the kind of thing that's in there. It sounds weird."

"It is unusual, but some of it is very well done. She definitely has talent."

When they got to the gallery, they stopped for a moment to look at what was in the front window.

"Weird," Trudy said, giving the tribal bust of Shakespeare a puzzled look. "But, yeah, I see what you mean about her having talent. I'm eager to see what's inside."

"No customers," Priscilla said, peering past the window display and into the gallery itself. She opened the door so she and Trudy could go inside.

Rayne came from the studio at the sound of the bell on the door, smiling as she wiped her hands on a paint rag and then on the men's dress shirt she wore for a smock.

"Priscilla, hello. Forgive my not shaking hands, but you don't want to get yellow ocher on you."

Priscilla chuckled. "No, thank you very much. I was telling my cousin Trudy about your gallery, and she really wanted to have a look around. I hope we're not interrupting you too much."

"Another cousin?" Rayne said. "It's good to meet you, Trudy."

"Thanks." Trudy looked around the gallery. "I'm impressed. Joan told me you had a lot of interesting things here."

"Is Joan your cousin too?" Rayne asked.

"My sister, actually, but we also have another cousin. Gail. Joan's really the only artist in the family, but we all like to look."

"You're more than welcome," Rayne said.

Priscilla unbuttoned her coat. "I thought there would be more people in here on a Friday."

"Friday afternoons are usually pretty slow." Rayne shrugged, looking amused and a little rueful at the same time. "If you want the truth, it's always a little slow. It's not easy getting established in this business."

"I think you have a lot of talent."

Rayne's full lips turned up at the corners. "Thank you, Priscilla. Too bad not much of my original stuff sells. Not that often anyway. But I have a lot of cute plaster molds, and I can dress the sculptures up to order. As Calvin says, those nickels and dimes do add up. And, of course, it helps to have a patron of the arts pitching in when needed."

Priscilla raised her eyebrows. "A patron? Wow, that must be nice."

"Don't be too impressed," Rayne said with a soft laugh. "It's just my husband, Donovan. He's an investment banker, so at least one of us has a steady income."

Priscilla chuckled. "You must enjoy being here in the summer when there are a lot of tourists."

"Oh, definitely. I didn't realize when we moved here that it would be so quiet in the wintertime."

"Haven't you been here long?" Priscilla asked.

"About eight months."

"It does get quiet in the winter," Trudy said, looking up from the sculpture of the woman with the scene of the dilapidated Paris café. "This is sad. Like she's remembering a man she's not with anymore."

Rayne gave her an enigmatic smile.

Priscilla studied the sculpture again herself. "From what I've seen, everything here makes you think. But I guess that's what art does."

"It should," Rayne said.

"Is all this your original work?" Trudy asked. "I heard you had some new things from an importer."

Rayne glanced briefly at Priscilla. "That's true, though most of what's on display here is mine."

"Will you put out the imported items soon?" Priscilla asked, now that Trudy had subtly given her an opening. "I'd love to see them."

"Actually, most of them are already spoken for. The importer has a number of buyers in the area, and they've already claimed the items."

"If he already had buyers, I'm surprised he cut you in on the deal."

Rayne looked at her for a moment, and Priscilla wondered if she had said too much too soon, but then Rayne shrugged again.

"I guess he'd rather not have to deal with sales tax and credit card companies and everything that has to do with selling to the final buyer. He says what he pays me is worth not having to worry about all that, and I'm pretty happy with the arrangement. Besides getting paid for handling the transactions, it brings people into the gallery. Who knows whether they might find something of mine they like too?"

"Sounds like a good deal for everyone," Priscilla said.

"He must be a nice guy." Trudy smiled guilelessly. "What's he like?"

"He's all right," Rayne said, wiping her hands again before she pushed a lock of curly hair behind her ear. "Always polite and never tries to take liberties like some men do. He told me about his wife once."

Trudy's eyebrows went up.

"But she died several years ago," Rayne added. "He said your cousin Joan reminds him a little of her. I think he must be pretty lonely, you know?"

"Sounds like it," Priscilla said. "That's too bad."

"Priscilla told me he imports things from all over." Trudy looked appealingly at Rayne. "What kinds of things does he bring in? Do you think we could see?"

Rayne chuckled. "I suppose so. It's not like I have other customers to wait on. Just remember, it's all spoken for, so don't get too attached to it."

"Oh, don't worry," Trudy said as she and Priscilla followed Rayne into her studio. "My husband would kill me if I spent the kind of money it would take to buy something from here."

"Not everything is expensive." Rayne showed Trudy the handcrafted items she had from South America. "Even this latest shipment is reasonably priced. At least in fine art circles."

She took them over to a stack of wooden crates in the corner and lifted the top off one. Inside, packed in straw, were five earthenware vessels, large, round-bellied, brownish-red pots with very narrow necks. She pulled the straw away from one of them, so Priscilla and Trudy could get a better look. It was made in the shape of a long-necked bird.

"I'd rather not take it out, if you don't mind," Rayne said. "The buyer wouldn't be very happy if it ended up getting damaged."

Trudy frowned.

"It's no problem," Priscilla said before she could object. "Is that what's in all the boxes?"

"To be honest, I'm not sure," Rayne admitted. "But I'd be surprised if they were all the same. Calvin always brings in things from native craftsmen who make everything by hand, so there's a lot of variety even from the same artist."

"That makes sense." Priscilla gestured toward the stack of crates. "Is this everything you'll be handling for him?"

"Oh, goodness, no. There's a lot more on his boat, but he probably won't bring it ashore until early next week. He told me he was due a little bit of a vacation and he's taking the holidays off." Rayne smiled at both of them. "Sounds like he wants to get to know Joan a little better."

Before Priscilla could respond, she noticed Trudy looking at something over her shoulder, and she turned around to the archway that separated the studio from the gallery. Standing just a few feet away from them was a tall, elegant-looking woman who might have been in her forties. Her hair and eyes were obsidian black, her skin a rich mahogany. Her teeth were gleaming white as she smiled.

CHAPTER FOUR

I'm sorry," the stranger said, the words carrying only the slightest trace of a Spanish accent. "I didn't mean to interrupt, but I didn't see anyone in the front of the shop."

"I didn't hear anyone come in," Rayne said, smiling in return. "And it's no interruption, we were just chatting. Is there something I can help you with?"

The woman came closer, her spike heels clicking on the studio's cement floor. "I have been told that you deal in Peruvian art. Do you have some I might see?"

"I do sell some from time to time. Actually, I've handled items from all over South and Central America, but right now I'm afraid I don't have anything but a few knickknacks. Most of them are from Peru, but some are from Chile and Ecuador." Rayne showed her the shelf with the native dolls and pottery. "They're not really anything for a serious collector, but I would guess you already knew that."

Again the woman smiled. "True. I've seen this sort of thing all my life. And I have to admit, they bring back fond memories."

"Am I right in thinking you're from South America?" Priscilla asked.

"From Lima," the woman said, holding out her hand. "I am Alessandra Alvarez. I've been in the United States for many years now, but I still miss my mountains and ocean breezes. I thought it would be nice to bring a little bit of home home with me."

Priscilla shook her hand and introduced herself and then Trudy.

"And I suppose you must be the Rayne Forster of the Rayne Forster Gallery," Alessandra said, shaking hands with Rayne too. "It is certainly a pleasure to meet you."

Rayne looked a little flustered. Priscilla was sure she didn't often get treated like a celebrity.

"I'm just sorry I don't have anything to show you," Rayne said, taking a step toward the gallery. "If you'd like me to speak to my importer, I'd be happy to ask him to find something especially for you on his next trip to Peru."

"That would be very kind of you." Alessandra didn't turn to follow her into the gallery. Instead, she moved a few steps closer to the crate full of pots that Rayne had shown Priscilla and Trudy a few minutes before. "But what about these? If I'm not mistaken, those are Shipibo."

Rayne's eyes lit. "Why, yes, they are. My importer bought those directly from some of the Shipibo women from the Ucayali River."

Alessandra nodded. "I'm familiar with their designs. I'd love to buy some of these. And don't worry, I won't quibble with you about the price. These are excellent."

"I'm sorry." Rayne swiftly packed the straw back around the exposed pot and slid the crate lid back into place. "These are all spoken for already."

Alessandra blinked at her, her red lips turned down at the corners. "All of them?"

"I'm afraid so. But, as I said, I'd be happy to have my importer find something specifically for you next time he goes to Peru. I believe he plans to make another trip down next month. Would that work for you?"

"There's not one piece in any of those crates that I could buy?"

"No," Rayne said. "I'm very sorry. If you'd like, you could leave me your phone number and I could call you if something becomes available."

Alessandra took out an expensive-looking engraved case and took out a business card. "I would certainly appreciate it. Or would it be possible for me to speak to your importer myself? If he were to bring back something specifically for me, I'd like to tell him more about what I want."

There was a fleeting look of displeasure on Rayne's expressive face, but it was almost instantly gone, replaced by a determinedly pleasant firmness. "I will pass your information along to him, though I'm not sure he'll get back to you right away. I think he's taking a few days off for Christmas."

"I'm not in a hurry," Alessandra said. "I'm taking a little bit of a break myself." She started to walk back into the gallery and then stopped. "What is your importer's name, may I ask? I'm wondering if he's someone I've dealt with before."

"Actually, it's better if I let him contact you when he's ready. Would that be okay?"

Alessandra gave a gracious nod of her head and then, bidding them all good afternoon, went into the gallery and out the front door.

Rayne looked after her, mouth taut, then she smiled apologetically at Priscilla and Trudy. "I hate when people do that. They think they can save a few bucks by dealing directly with the importer. And, yes, I suppose they could, but I'm sure not going to cut my own throat by making it easy for them."

"Maybe Calvin will still have her go through you on anything he brings back for her," Priscilla said, looking toward the door that led out to the street. "She certainly sounds like she knows what she's talking about."

Rayne narrowed her eyes. "She does that."

"Anyway," Trudy said brightly, "you were telling us about this friend of yours, the importer."

Rayne's taut expression softened into a smile. "I don't know if you'd call us friends precisely, but he seems like a nice enough guy. I don't have any complaints."

"You mentioned he told you about his wife," Priscilla said. "Joan did tell me that he was a widower."

"Yes, he said she passed away several years ago. I can't help feeling a little sorry for him."

"That is sad." Priscilla looked at the crates one more time, trying to see if there was anything on them that would tell her something about Calvin. "He must have a fairly large boat if he carries his own cargo."

Rayne shrugged. "I haven't seen it. He says it's a yacht, but I don't know anything else about it. He brings everything here in a van. I suppose he rents it while he's on the island."

"You're sure his wife is dead?" Trudy asked suspiciously.

Rayne laughed softly. "I haven't researched it, no, but that's what he told me. I don't have any reason not to believe him. Maybe you should ask your sister about him. If they're an item, she ought to know more than I do."

"Oh, we're just being nosy," Priscilla said airily, but she gave Trudy a warning look behind Rayne's back. "We really just wanted to have a look around here since I was telling Trudy about my visit earlier this week. I don't know how we both managed to miss the place since you've been here for months."

"I hope you'll both come back," Rayne told them as she walked them to the door. "I've enjoyed the company."

"It was good to meet you," Trudy said.

"Thanks for having us," Priscilla added. "We'll try to not be such pests next time we visit."

Rayne laughed and waved as Priscilla and Trudy turned up their coat collars and headed out into the cold.

"That wasn't all that helpful," Trudy said once they were back in the SUV.

Priscilla turned on the engine and let the car warm up a little before pulling onto the street. "Well, we found out he has a yacht. It's a start."

"We don't even know the name of the yacht!" Trudy protested.

"I don't know if that really matters, does it?"

"All right, fine," Trudy grumbled. "We'll just wait and see what Joan tells us. Maybe she'll even invite us to the wedding!"

"Now you're just being silly. Now what if, instead of sticking our noses in where they're not wanted, we do something helpful for somebody?"

"I guess that would be nice."

"Would you like to help me make some casseroles and a few other goodies we can take over to Gerald's daughter's house?" Priscilla told Trudy the little she knew about Gerald's grandbaby. "I thought we could make some meals that Aggie could put in the freezer for when she doesn't feel like cooking for the family. What do you say?"

"Well, sure! That poor baby! And poor Gerald!"

They drove back to Priscilla's cottage and went through her cookbooks, picking out a few favorite freezable recipes and then jotting down the ingredients they'd need to make some of them. After that they went to Ortmann's to buy what Priscilla didn't already have.

"Wow!" Trudy said once they had carried everything out to the SUV. "That was quite a total! Are you sure I can't chip in?"

"Oh, no." Priscilla glanced at the grocery bags in the back seat. It had ended up costing more than she expected. "No, it was my idea. If you'll just help me prepare everything, that'll be a huge help."

This was little enough to do. She drove away from the store, unable to imagine facing the kind of medical expenses Gerald's family was likely to have. How in the world would they manage? There had to be more she could do herself to help them. *God*, she prayed silently, *what can I do? How can I help?*

"...to your house?"

Priscilla blinked, suddenly realizing that Trudy was speaking to her. "I'm sorry, what?"

"I said aren't we going to your house? I thought we were going to cook."

Priscilla realized she had missed her turn. "Sorry about that. I guess I was miles away."

She turned at the next street and headed in the direction of the lighthouse.

Priscilla and Trudy spent the rest of the afternoon making meatloaf and chicken noodle casserole and turkey pot pie among other things. When they had everything packed up and ready to go, Priscilla called Gerald and left a message on his cell phone. He returned her call a few minutes later.

"Hi. What's up?"

He sounded rushed.

"Hi," Priscilla said. "I just wanted to let you know Trudy and I have been making some food for Aggie. You know, things she can put in the freezer for whenever she doesn't have time to cook. Do you think she'd like that?"

"Hey, that'd be great! I know she and Nick have been living off burgers and tacos the past few days. They'd love some home cooking."

"Good. Is there a good time we could take it over to her? Or should I give her a call directly? I just didn't want to bother her right now."

"No, I'm sure it wouldn't be a bother," Gerald said. "She'll love you for what you're doing. But since I'm on my way over there anyway, why don't I stop by your place and pick the stuff up? Then you won't have to get out."

"That would be perfect," Priscilla said. "I'll be watching for you."

"Hi." Priscilla opened the door for Gerald. "Can you come in for a while?"

"I'm sorry, no," he said. His eyes looked tired.

"Well, at least come inside so I can shut the door." She smiled at him. "I can't afford to heat the whole neighborhood."

He managed a bit of a grin and followed her into the kitchen where Trudy was packing up some paper plates and plastic tableware. "Hi, Trudy. Thanks for helping with all this."

"I'm happy to do it," Trudy said, "but it was all Priscilla's idea."

"Well, thanks to both of you. Aggie and Nick will be very grateful."

"Can't you sit down for just a minute?" Priscilla asked. "I can make coffee."

Gerald shook his head. "Aggie's expecting me. Is there something in particular you wanted to talk about?"

"No." Priscilla suddenly wished Trudy wasn't there to over-hear her every word. "I was just wondering how you're doing. How's the baby?"

"She's doing all right. Aggie and Nick are hanging in there."

"How about you?"

Gerald didn't answer right away. "I'm...doing okay. Trying to work out some things financially."

"What are you going to do?"

"I don't know yet. We don't have any real information from the insurance company and the hospital yet, but I'm trying to think about what we might do to get through this." He leaned against the counter and drew a deep breath. "I just have to trust God to figure this out and do what I can."

"Of course," Priscilla murmured. "Still, it would be good to know how this will all work out. It's got to be so hard not knowing."

That made him chuckle. "Tell me about it. But I have some ideas. I don't want you to be worrying about this too. It's not your problem."

"I still want to help."

"I know." He gave Priscilla a look that made her feel warm all over. "We all appreciate that."

"And we're praying for you," Trudy said as she handed him the accessories she had packed up, her voice softer than usual.

"Thanks," Gerald said gruffly, then he cleared his throat. "Okay, so where's this feast you've prepared?"

Trudy giggled, and they all carried everything out to the white Coast Guard SUV he was driving. When it was all secured, he told

Priscilla he'd call her when he got a chance. She couldn't help sighing as he drove away.

"Well, that was quick," Trudy said, one hand on her hip.

"You can't blame him for wanting to spend time with his family right now," Priscilla told her as they hurried back into the warmth of the cottage. And she didn't blame him. Not at all. She just wished he would let her be there with him.

CHAPTER FIVE

She didn't hear from Gerald the next day. And on the day after that, Sunday, he had been preoccupied at church, staying only long enough afterward to ask for prayer for his daughter and granddaughter before hurrying off to be with them. He hadn't told Priscilla anything more than he had before, that they were still waiting for more information. But late that afternoon, he called her on the phone.

"Hey."

"Hey, yourself." His voice sounded thick, a little rough.

"How are things?" She carried the phone over to the couch and sat down in front of the fire.

"They're good. I—" He cleared his throat. "Sorry about that. Sammy and I just had a nap."

He must not have been sleeping as well at night as he had claimed he would. He hadn't ever mentioned taking a nap during the day.

"I hope it was a good one. How's Aggie holding up? And Nick?"

"Oh, they said to tell you thank you for all the food. Aggie was so relieved to not have to think about what to do for dinner, I thought she was going to start crying."

"I hope you told them Trudy and I were happy to do it. But how are they?"

"Oh, you know," he said. "They're trying hard. Putting a brave face on it. Ava's just a little ray of sunshine, like always. Aggie wants to hold her all the time now, but she's not having it. She's got to get down and play."

"That's good to hear. Kids are pretty resilient most of the time, no matter how badly they scare everybody else. How's Max handling everything?"

"He's trying to be brave, but he's old enough to know Mommy and Daddy are worried about his baby sister. We're all trying to make sure he doesn't feel like he's been forgotten in all this too."

"Good. Poor little thing. So what are you doing for the rest of the day?"

Gerald sighed. "Nothing, I guess. I thought I'd take Sammy for a walk and then do some stuff around the house. I've put things off the past couple of days."

"Would you like some company? Jake and I could use a little exercise too." Priscilla smiled as her dog lifted his ears at the sound of his name. "No, wait. I just had a better idea. Why don't we take Sammy and Jake to the pond with us while we skate? That way we can both get out of the house, get a little fresh air, and just have some fun. I found my skates buried in the front closet this morning. What do you think?"

He let out a heavy breath. "You know, Priscilla—"

"No, it's all right. It's a dumb idea. You've got a lot on your mind—"

"I was about to say that's the best idea I've heard all day."

Priscilla was glad he wasn't able to see the sappy grin that was suddenly plastered to her face. "Okay, uh, when would be a good time?"

"How about now?" he said, "but we'll have to walk the dogs first and leave them at home. They aren't allowed at the pond. Besides, I'm thinking it might not be a good idea to walk a dog on skates." He laughed. "That could end badly."

"I see your point." Priscilla laughed with him. "We'll both have a quick walk and then...?"

"How about I come pick you up? Say half an hour?"

"That's perfect. And you could come to dinner and then help me finish off the Lane Cake."

"Dinner? That would be great."

"There's still plenty of cake, and I was planning to make a meatloaf. Nothing fancy, but you're welcome."

"That would be about the best thing ever. I haven't even thought about what I'm going to do tonight. I'm sure I'm nearly out of everything to cook with. Is there anything I can bring over? I don't mind going to the store."

"Just bring your appetite."

"I'd better get moving" he said. "We don't want to wait till it's too dark and cold to be out. It's a little overcast now, but I think we'll be all right for a while. Then I can come help you fix dinner or whatever else needs doing around your place."

"Deal. But the best thing you can do for me is just relax for the afternoon, okay? I've managed to make meatloaf more than once before, and I did it all by myself."

That made him chuckle. "Okay. And I really appreciate it."

"You're more than welcome. See you in a little bit."

Less than an hour later, Priscilla and Gerald were walking up to Uncle Seth's Pond, bundled up and carrying their ice skates. As always, Gerald's heavy wool coat hung open in front.

"I don't know how you don't freeze," she said, tugging her knitted cap down lower over her ears.

"In this? Not a chance. You ought to try being out in the North Atlantic this time of year."

UNCLE SETH'S POND
This beach was given to the Town of
West Tisbury for the use and enjoyment
of its residents. Please observe the rules
and respect the privacy of neighbors.

NO PARKING BETWEEN SIGNS
SOAPS PROHIBITED
NO ANIMALS ⁓ NO FIRES
NO LOUD NOISES
CARRY IN ⁓ CARRY OUT
USE AT OWN RISK

Priscilla smiled as she read the fading sign. "You were right about the dogs. But what a lovely gift to the town."

The pond was a circle of silver surrounded by leafless, snow-laden trees. Couples and families were circling the pond, talking and laughing and trying to stay out of the way of the impromptu hockey game taking place in the center. Priscilla and Gerald watched for a moment or two and then sat on a nearby bench to lace up their skates.

"I told you I'm not very good at this," she said, getting precariously to her feet.

"Don't worry, I'll help you." He put her arm through his. "We'll take it slow."

They didn't say much, and after a few shaky moments, she found she wasn't as inept as she had feared. Gerald seemed happy just to not be by himself, and Priscilla was glad to give him whatever support he needed. If he wanted to talk, she'd listen, and if he wanted to be quiet, that was okay too. It was a comfortable silence, and the fresh beauty of the afternoon was enough.

For a while, she prayed as they skated, silently asking God to be with Gerald and his family, to give them wisdom about what to do and to provide for their needs and to please heal little Ava. Later, when Gerald was still silent, her thoughts drifted to the dinner she was about to prepare and whether she still had enough fresh vegetables to make a salad.

"Would you like to have—"

When she suddenly broke off, Gerald followed her glance to a couple skating about fifty feet ahead of them. "Is that the guy? Gallico?"

She nodded. "I don't think they've seen us yet. I sure would like for you to meet him, just to see what you think of him. I don't want to get in the middle of something that's none of my business, so if you say he's all right, I'll take your word for it."

"It's hard to tell much about a guy from just being introduced. What do you think? Do you want to see if they'll come have dinner with us? I know that's not what you'd originally planned, but it would give us both a chance to get to know him a little. Maybe you'll feel different about him. If not, maybe you'll know why you don't trust him."

"Are you sure that's all right with you? I thought you'd rather relax for the evening."

He grinned and shrugged. "I wouldn't mind something to take my mind off everything that's going on with Ava. And maybe this will be a quick, easy way to set your mind at ease about Joan. Sounds like a win-win to me. " He narrowed his eyes, looking at Calvin. "Do you have enough to feed everybody?"

"Plenty."

"All right, then. I'm ready to be introduced."

He offered Priscilla his arm, and they skated up to the other couple. Bright eyed and rosy cheeked, Joan was laughing at something Calvin was telling her and didn't notice them until they were beside her.

"Hello." Priscilla smiled at her cousin. "I didn't know you'd be here."

"You either." Joan looked around the frozen pond. "Isn't it beautiful?"

"Lovely."

Calvin nodded at Priscilla. "Good to see you again. Who's your friend?"

"Oh." Joan turned just a little pink. "Let me introduce you two. Gerald, this is Calvin Gallico. Calvin, this is Gerald O'Bannon."

"Gerald's got an Irish setter named Sammy," Priscilla put in. "We were going to walk our dogs, but then we decided coming here would be a little more fun."

The two men shook hands.

"Good to meet you," Calvin said with his usual generous grin. "Seems like everybody's a dog owner but me. Not that I don't love the little fellas, like one sweet little blue heeler I know." He squeezed Joan's hand. "But being on my boat for days and weeks on end and roaming around all over the world, I don't really have a lot of time for one."

"Oh, I don't know," Gerald said. "A lot of dogs enjoy the sea. Sammy sure enjoys it when we go out on my boat."

Calvin glanced at Joan. "Who knows? Maybe someday I'll have one come along with me on the *Barrett*."

"So that one's yours," Gerald said as they all started skating again. "I've seen her in the harbor. She's a beauty. Kind of tough living out there this time of year though, isn't it?"

"Not so bad. Not so bad. As long as you don't mind not having running water and using space heaters and electric blankets. I've got bubblers to keep the hull from freezing, and on a sunny day the shrink wrap makes the deck as good as a tropical beach."

Gerald smiled, nodding, but Priscilla was only puzzled.

"Shrink wrap?"

"It's a plastic cover that goes over the cockpit and hull," Gerald explained, "to keep out the moisture."

"You'll have to come out on her sometime," Calvin said, and he looked at Joan once more. "I thought it might be nice if I met some of Joan's friends and family. Nothing fancy of course, just so we can all get to know each other. What do you say, Joanie?"

Joan's eyebrows went up, but she managed a smile. Priscilla couldn't remember anyone ever calling her Joanie.

"Uh, sure. That would be fun." Joan smiled tentatively at Priscilla. "You'd come, wouldn't you?"

"Of course I would," Priscilla said. "In fact, Gerald and I wanted to catch up with you because we thought it might be nice if the two of you came over to my house for dinner tonight. You don't have any plans, do you?"

"Well..."

"That would be great," Calvin said for her. "We hadn't really talked about dinner yet. I mean, I was going to see if Joan would go out with me, but I wasn't sure if she was already tired of having me around, you know?"

Joan's cheeks turned pinker than the wind had already made them. "Nothing of the kind."

"So what do you think? It would be a little less intimidating if I could get to know just a couple of people at first. Then when we have our little party on the yacht, I could talk to somebody besides you, right?"

"I guess so." Joan looked up at Priscilla, her dark eyes uncertain. "If it's not too much trouble."

"No trouble at all. You're always welcome, you know that, and we'd love to get to know Calvin better." She smiled appealingly at the man. "Now, it's nothing fancy. I hadn't really planned on any-one coming over at all, but then I invited Gerald and we saw you over here and, well, now we have a dinner party."

"You don't let that worry you at all, Priscilla," Calvin said. "Joanie already told me you were a great cook. I'm sure whatever you fix will be first class."

"I'll try." Priscilla slowed to a stop, seeing they were back at the bench where they had left their shoes. "What would all of you like to do? It'll take me a while to cook. Do you want to come over now and just visit until dinner's ready? Or would you like to come when it's time to eat?"

"I'm good either way," Calvin said cheerfully.

Joan looked at her watch. "I think I ought to get home and feed Sister and get tidied up. What if we come over in about an hour?"

"That would work." Priscilla turned to Gerald. "Are you about ready to go?"

"Yeah, we probably should." Gerald nodded at Calvin. "Good to meet you."

"Yeah." Calvin's smile was wide. "You too. See you soon."

"He doesn't seem all that sinister to me," Gerald said softly as he and Priscilla removed their skates and put their shoes back on.

She huffed. "I never said that. Do you want to come over while I cook?"

"I'd better get tidied up too." He smiled into her eyes. "This was a great idea though. Just getting away from the house and out into the air was exactly what I needed."

"I'm glad."

He took her back home and escorted her up to her door.

"Come back soon," she told him. "I want you to have as long as possible to talk to Calvin and see what you think."

"I'll do it."

He waved as he drove away.

Not quite an hour later, there was a knock at Priscilla's door. It was Joan.

"Hi," she said, looking more like a little brown bird than usual all bundled up against the cold.

"Come in before you freeze," Priscilla told her, and then she looked both ways down the street. "Where's Calvin?"

"He said he had a few quick things to take care of, but he'd be here in a few minutes." Joan followed Priscilla into the kitchen and poured herself a cup of coffee. "Wasn't it fun out on the pond? I haven't been skating for years, but I guess I still remembered how."

"I felt the same way, but it was so nice to be out there, and everything was so beautiful."

Joan shivered a little and warmed her hands on her cup. "I don't know how we all didn't freeze, but it didn't seem that cold when we were skating, did it?"

"We were having fun," Priscilla said warmly.

Joan took a deep drink of her coffee and then looked at Priscilla. "No Gerald yet?"

"He's on his way, I'm sure. Would you put these biscuits in the pan for me? I'm sorry they're just from a can, but at least they're quick."

"Sure." Joan cracked the can of biscuits on the edge of the countertop, making it pop, and then began arranging them in the pan Priscilla got out for her. "And no need to apologize. I love this kind. So does Calvin."

Priscilla peeked in on the nicely browning meatloaf. "That's good to know," she said, making sure to keep any hint of concern out of her voice, reminding herself she had no identifiable reason to doubt him. "How did that come up?"

Joan passed her the pan of biscuits and then opened the silverware drawer. "Want me to set the table?"

"That'd be great." Priscilla put the biscuits in the oven.

"Calvin came over for dinner Friday night. I burned a pan of my homemade rolls and had to use some of the canned ones instead." Joan began laying out the forks and knives and spoons. "But he said he loved them."

"Sounds like he's easy to get along with."

Joan stopped what she was doing. "Do you think it's too soon for me to have already invited him to dinner?"

Priscilla laughed lightly. "Maybe *you* do."

Joan sighed. "Maybe I do."

Priscilla got out some plates and glasses and started helping her lay the table, waiting for her to say more if she wanted to.

"We met before Thanksgiving," Joan said finally. "At Rayne's like I told you. I didn't think much of it. He said something funny, I can't remember what now, and then told me I had a nice laugh. Do you know how long it's been since a man gave me a compliment?"

Priscilla knew she wasn't actually looking for an answer, but she did know how it was for women "of a certain age." It was easy to feel invisible.

Joan folded some napkins and put them under the forks. "Anyway, I didn't see him again until the next Saturday. He was going into Carter's to buy some screws for one of his chairs that had a wobbly leg, and we said hello again. Then we ended up having breakfast, well, brunch really, at the Nautilus Café. Then the next time I saw him was when you and I were at Rayne's last Tuesday. So there's just not that much to tell."

"And you had lunch," Priscilla said.

"Yes, we went to Walt's and had a burger. He was on his way to talk to a buyer, but when he found out I hadn't eaten yet that day either, he insisted that I come with him. It was really very thoughtful, don't you think?"

"Very considerate."

"There's just not that much to it. Maybe he's a little lonely." Joan smiled faintly. "Maybe I am too. Once in a while anyway. Is there anything wrong with being friends with somebody?"

"Of course not," Priscilla said, feeling a trifle foolish herself.

"Then why do I feel like a teenager who's been sneaking out of the house to run around town with the school bad boy?"

Priscilla giggled. "He doesn't quite seem the bad-boy type, does he?"

"Not really. But he does make me feel a little like a girl again. I know it's nothing serious, but I like it. What's wrong with that?"

Priscilla hugged her. "Not a thing."

The doorbell rang just as the oven timer dinged.

Priscilla glanced toward the living room. "Do me a favor and answer it, will you? I have to get dinner out of the oven."

Joan wiped her hands on the dishtowel by the sink, smoothed her hair, then went to the door. A moment later she brought both Calvin and Gerald into the kitchen.

"Perfect timing," Priscilla told them as she set the meatloaf and rolls on the table. "Joan, can you get the green beans and corn off the stove? Then we can go ahead and sit down."

"Smells delicious," Gerald said as he removed his coat and hat and put them in an empty chair.

Calvin removed his fedora and heavy jacket and put them with Gerald's things. Then he handed Priscilla a square, shallow box. "Thanks for having me, Priscilla. I thought maybe you'd like those."

"That's very nice of you," she said and, shaking the box slightly, she smiled. "If I was guessing, I'd say you've been to Ben and Bill's."

She opened the box to reveal a delicious-looking assortment of gourmet chocolates.

He nodded modestly. "I understand Ben and Bill's is one of your favorites."

"Definitely. And we'll all have some after dinner if you'd like, though there's cake too."

"I don't know," he said. "The way that dinner smells, I may not end up having room for even one extra bite."

"I'll let you be the judge of that."

Priscilla was happy to see that everyone seemed to enjoy the meal, and the conversation was light and pleasant. She had worried about how to get Calvin to tell her more about himself, but eventually she began to think that getting him to stop talking would be by far the more difficult task.

"The meatloaf was great," Calvin said, pushing back his chair from his empty plate. "My wife, God rest her, wasn't much of a cook, but she did have a way with meatloaf. Yours is the closest to hers I've ever had."

"I'll take that as a compliment," Priscilla said, "though I'm sorry about your wife. I lost my husband a couple of years ago."

"That's too bad." Calvin smiled across the table at Joan. "That's one thing Joanie and I have in common. People who haven't faced the death of a loved one don't really understand what it's like."

Priscilla looked at Gerald. Each of the four of them had lost a spouse. Gerald's loss was through divorce, not death, but it had been a loss all the same and perhaps in many ways more painful.

"But eventually you have to move on," Calvin added. "Am I right?"

Gerald nodded. "Were you married long?"

"Seventeen years," Calvin told him. "I'm no spring chicken, as you can see readily enough. We had a long time together and she stood by me through a lot, but she's been gone about five years now."

"You never married again?" Priscilla asked.

Calvin shook his head. "But who knows? Maybe I'll change my mind someday." There was a sudden glint of humor in his eyes as he looked over at Joan. "I didn't know Martha's Vineyard had so many sights worth seeing."

Joan looked down at her plate, a little flustered but smiling.

"Your wife must have been relatively young," Priscilla said.

Calvin's expression was suddenly grim. "Cancer doesn't care,"

No one said anything for a minute after that. Priscilla couldn't help thinking about her own late husband, also a victim of cancer. It wasn't an easy loss, she knew far too well. Surely Calvin had a right to a second chance at love as much as anyone else did.

"Tough break," Gerald said finally. "I'm sorry."

Calvin shrugged. "You pick up and go on, like I said."

Gerald took a moment to stir his coffee and then take a sip. "I hear you travel all over looking for things to import. That must be an interesting way to live."

Calvin shoveled in the last bite of his second slice of meatloaf and then waved his fork in Gerald's direction. "I wouldn't trade for it. No question. There's nothing better than being out there on the water. You should try it sometime."

Gerald chuckled and took the last biscuit. "I do, just about every day."

"Oh yeah?"

"I'm Coast Guard."

Calvin coughed suddenly, then took a drink of water. "Sorry about that. Swallowed the wrong way. I shouldn't try to talk and eat at the same time." He wiped his mouth on his napkin. "Anyhow, Coast Guard. That's great. I hate to think what would happen to a guy like me without you folks out there looking after us. There are a lot of bad guys around and lots of ocean for them to hide in. You been in the Coast Guard long?"

"Over twenty years."

"Nice. You must have seen about everything out there."

"Pretty much," Gerald assured him. "And what I haven't seen I've heard about. Though you've probably seen and heard a thing or two, traveling all over the way you do."

Calvin chuckled. "I have that. I guess part of what I like about this business is getting to see all the sights and meet a lot of different people and then bring some of what I've seen back here for other people to enjoy."

"And tell all your stories too," Joan put in. "I think that's the best part."

"Rayne let us see one of your Peruvian pots," Priscilla said.

"Oh, yeah?" Calvin frowned. "I hope she was careful with it. She knows I've already got buyers for all of those things."

"She told us," Priscilla assured him. "And she didn't take it out of the crate or anything. She just let us peek at it."

He smiled. "Nice, aren't they? I don't know which piece you saw, but they're all good. Mostly made by the Shipibo people down there."

"That reminds me," she said. "Did Rayne tell you there was someone in her gallery on Friday who was interested in that stuff?"

"Really?"

"Rayne told her it was all sold."

Calvin frowned. "Her?"

"Yes. She said she was originally from Peru herself. She was asking if you had more pottery like that on your boat."

"What did Rayne tell her?"

Joan looked faintly startled at the tautness in his voice. Gerald's eyes narrowed.

Calvin grinned suddenly. "Heh, you know how it is. People see something they like and then think you can hop over to South America or Africa or wherever and pick up another one just like it. That's why I try to get gallery owners to handle the actual business transactions for me and all the red tape that goes with it, taxes and all the paperwork and fussy customers and everything else. It's well worth the cut I give them. Anyhow, I'd like to know if I'm going to have to deal with her myself or if Rayne took care of it."

"She told the woman she'd give you her information and let you contact her if you were interested in bringing back something specific for her," Priscilla told him. "That's all I know."

"She shouldn't have told her that. I might not be back in Peru or even in South America for months. That's why I don't do special requests. I don't like to have to be in a particular place at a particular time if I can help it." He winked at Joan. "Unless I have a particularly good reason, that is."

"I hope you make a good profit on what you've brought in this time," Joan said, "and enjoy yourself while you're here. That's reason enough, isn't it?"

"There are a lot of nice reasons to visit Martha's Vineyard," he told her.

Priscilla gave Gerald a wary glance. The man was laying it on way too thick.

When everyone had finished eating, she served cake and coffee from the Hoosier cabinet in the dining room, and then they all went into the living room to chat in front of the fire. Before long, Calvin yawned and checked his watch.

"Well, I'd better get going. I have some business to take care of before it gets too late."

"I'd better get home too," Joan added.

When they were gone, Priscilla and Gerald sat in the living room a while longer.

"What do you think?" she asked, clutching the plate holding her barely tasted piece of cake.

Gerald frowned. "I don't know. He didn't actually say anything wrong, but I see what you mean about him. He's just...too much. He's too friendly. Tries too hard. If I didn't know what a short time they'd known each other, I'd swear he was about ready to pop the question with Joan."

"I know. I don't want to meddle, but it just feels weird to me. Is that enough of a reason for her not to be friends with the man?"

Gerald shrugged. "It's not a very tangible one anyway."

"So what, if anything, do we do?"

Gerald stood up and held out his hand for her plate. "You done with that?"

She handed it to him and then let him help her to her feet.

"What we do first is see to the dishes."

"That would be very helpful of you," she said. "Thank you. And then?"

"Then you let me do some checking up on one Calvin Gallico. I should be able to find out something tomorrow. Would that suit you?"

"That would be great."

As they did the dishes, they chatted about anything and everything—everything but Calvin Gallico. But on his way out afterward, Gerald stopped at the front door.

"I don't want you to worry, okay? I'll find out what I can about Gallico and let you know right away."

"Thank you. I know you have a lot on your mind, and I appreciate you looking into this for me."

"Happy to do it," he said. "It'll give me something to do to take my mind off Ava."

"Let me know how she's doing too, okay?"

"I will," he said, and then he hurried out to his car and drove away.

He called her late the next morning.

"Listen, I'm at work and don't have more than a minute, but I wanted to let you know what I found out about Calvin."

"Is it bad?"

"I suppose it could be worse. The most important part is that he spent five years in prison in California for trafficking in drugs."

CHAPTER SIX

Joan looked warily at Priscilla when she answered the door that afternoon.

"Thanks for letting me come over," Priscilla said, following her into the living room. "I know Mondays can be especially stressful at work."

Joan took her coat and let her warm herself before the fire. "You sounded as if you had something to say that couldn't wait."

"Joan." Priscilla took both of her hands, holding them tightly. "I'm really sorry. I don't like to tell you things I already know you don't want to hear."

"It's about Calvin, isn't it?" Joan shook her head in grim certainty. "Of course it is. You don't like my seeing him."

"Can we sit down?"

Priscilla urged her toward the sofa. Once they were seated, Joan's dog immediately jumped up beside them, panting happily in Priscilla's face. Why couldn't their lives be as simple as Sister's?

"Okay," Joan said. "So tell me."

Priscilla petted Sister for a moment. "First," she said finally, "I want you to know that I would be happy for you, very happy, if you found someone you cared about, someone who truly cares about you. But I don't want you to be hurt, and I don't want anyone taking advantage of you."

Joan merely looked at her, waiting for her to get to the point.

"You knew that already," Priscilla conceded. "Here it is, then. I found out that Calvin served time."

Joan pressed her lips together. "Do you mean he served five years in California for dealing drugs?"

"You know?"

"I do. He told me that almost first thing. He didn't want me to find out later and then be mad at him because he hadn't told me himself."

"Uh, okay. That doesn't bother you?"

Joan huffed. "Of course it bothers me. Drug dealers make money off of other people's misery and hopelessness. It's horrible. But Calvin got out of that life twenty years ago. After he served time, after his wife left him, after he ended up with no money, no home, no car, and no anything else, he decided it was time to do something that would maybe give him some better results." Her lips trembled slightly. "He said he had to hit bottom before he was desperate enough to ask for help, and he found that help in God. He gave his heart to the Lord, and it changed him totally. If God will give him a fresh start, why shouldn't we?"

"I'm glad to hear that," Priscilla admitted. "I don't know of anything else that would make someone like that really change."

"After that," Joan said, "the only job he could get was bussing tables at a diner. He worked his way up to manager. He got a car and a decent place to live. He even convinced his wife that he was serious about straightening out his life. He promised her he would never go back to dealing, that if she would give him just one more chance, just one, that he'd make her proud."

"Joan—"

"No, let me finish. I know it sounds cliché, but she gave him that chance and he did make her proud. He tried several different things and did all right with them, but it was when he started dealing with imports that he really became successful. They had a house on the ocean and everything was great." Joan bit her lip. "And then she died. He sold the house and everything else and bought the yacht. He spent a long time on the ocean, just by himself. He told me he never thought he would ever care about anybody but her until, well, until recently." There was pleading in her eyes now. "I know we haven't known each other long, and I'm not saying there's anything serious between us. There may never be. But I can't just tell him to go away."

"I understand that," Priscilla said. "I just want you to be careful. If he's involved in something illegal—"

"That was twenty years ago. How long is he supposed to pay for that mistake? What else does he have to do?"

Sister looked up at Joan, her little brows drawn together.

Priscilla stroked the puppy's head, calming her. "I'm not saying he should never be forgiven for whatever he's done, especially if he's a Christian now. I'm just saying you need to be aware of his history."

"I *am* aware. Or don't you think I'm capable of dealing with something like this without supervision?"

"No, I'm not saying that at all. Obviously, you already knew about this. And you're right. He served his time. He should be allowed to put that behind him and have the same chance at success as anyone else. But look at what he does."

"He's an importer. What's wrong with that?"

"But where does he import things from? South America. Huge amounts of drugs are smuggled into the country from there. Someone like him would have contacts. He'd know all about the business of distributing and selling."

Joan's mouth tightened. "That's not fair. You have zero evidence that he's doing anything of the kind. Just because he goes to South America, you immediately assume he's running drugs? What about when he goes to Africa? What's he smuggling in from there? Cheetahs? Rhinoceroses?"

"I'm sorry," Priscilla said gently. "I didn't mean to upset you. And, really, I'm not accusing him of anything. I just…I'm worried about you. I don't know him, and to be honest, neither do you."

"I realize that, but don't you think you're getting worried over nothing? You act like we're planning to elope next week."

"Because that's what *he's* acting like. Could he be any more obvious? Don't you think it's a little soon for that?"

Joan's face turned redder than it already was, and she ducked her head. "He's just being silly."

"He didn't sound silly to me."

"Well, maybe not silly, but kind. He's a little over the top, sure, but I don't think he means anything by it. He's just trying to be complimentary. It's nice of him. I'm not taking it seriously."

"Okay." Priscilla wasn't entirely convinced, but she didn't want to push things any further just now. "I think that's wise. If he's sincere, going slow won't hurt anything."

"I know that." Joan's mouth was set in a hard line. "I'm not a child or an idiot. I know the difference between right and wrong. I know enough not to rush into anything."

"I know," Priscilla told her. "I know. It's just that you're not used to this kind of thing, and—"

"And you are?"

Priscilla felt her own face heat. "No. You know I haven't dated that much, not even before Gary and I got married. I'm just worried that—"

"That I'm too stupid to run my own life?"

"Joan, no!"

Joan stood up. "Well, good. I'm glad you realize I can take care of myself. Was there anything else?"

"No, I–I guess not." Priscilla got to her feet. "Look, I'm sorry."

Joan breathed out heavily. "It's okay. I just had a rough morning at work, and I'd probably do better being left alone for a while, okay?"

"Sure. Call me if you want to talk or something. I enjoyed dinner and skating yesterday. I think we both did pretty good, don't you?"

"Good thing we went when we did," Joan said. "It's warmed up. The pond will be slush before long."

"I'm glad we didn't miss it." Priscilla gave Sister another pat, got her coat from the chair where Joan had laid it, and put it on. "See you later?"

"All right," Joan said. That was all.

Priscilla didn't feel any easier about the situation as she drove home from her cousin's house. All she had accomplished was making Joan mad at her. As hard as she had tried to be understanding and not pushy, she had still managed to make a mess of things. But if there was something going on with Calvin—

She gripped the steering wheel more tightly. "God, please show me what to do. If Calvin is doing something wrong, please bring it to light. Please protect Joan and all of us. And let her know that I wouldn't worry about her if I didn't love her."

She drove a little farther in silence and then pulled over to the side of the road and took out her cell phone.

"Trudy?" she said as soon as her call was answered. "Are you home?"

"Sure. What's wrong? Is it Joan?"

"No, nothing's actually wrong," Priscilla told her. "But it is about Joan and this Calvin guy. Would it be all right if I came over?"

"Of course! I'll be watching for you."

"What is it?" Trudy pressed the instant she opened her front door. "Come in, it's freezing."

She bustled Priscilla into her airy, modern living room, hurried her out of her coat, and sat with her on the comfy blue couch. The Christmas party was going to be at Trudy's again this year, and everything that could be decorated already was.

"Don't be in such a rush," Priscilla told her. "There's not a fire or anything."

Trudy's platinum curls bounced as she shook her head. "Maybe not, but I can tell when something's bothering you. What's going on? Do you want coffee?"

Priscilla paused. "No, I just had some at Joan's. Thank you, though."

"But what's wrong? Why were you at Joan's?"

"I just went to talk, okay?"

Trudy frowned. "Then what's wrong?"

"It's what I went to talk to her about." Priscilla took a deep breath. "Promise me you won't tell anybody this. Not anybody, all right?"

"But Dan—"

"If you tell Dan, he has to make sure not to tell anyone at all. Understand?"

"He wouldn't!"

"Yes, I know." Priscilla paused again, suddenly not sure if this was a good idea, but Trudy was Joan's sister. She would certainly want to help her.

"Well?"

"Gerald called me this morning," Priscilla said at last. "He told me that Calvin Gallico served five years in California for dealing drugs."

Trudy raised her eyebrows. "Oh!"

"He got out fifteen years ago, and I found out just a little while ago that Joan already knows about it."

Trudy looked anxious. "And he hasn't been in trouble since then?"

"Not anything that ended up on his record, according to Gerald. That might mean he went straight. Or it might just mean he's gotten smarter over the past few years."

"I hate to ask this, but what did Joan say?"

Priscilla winced. "She wasn't very happy about us checking him out."

"But what if he's still doing illegal stuff? What if he's actually dangerous? We can't just let something bad happen to her!"

"I know. That's why I thought I'd better come see you. I don't know exactly what we can do, but the more of us who are looking out for Joan, the better. Since Gerald's in the Coast Guard, he knows about dealing with smugglers and other bad people. We'll need him with us for sure."

"And Gail," Trudy said. "She'll want to help."

"Right. I just didn't want to bother her at work. But maybe we can get together for dinner or something and talk this out."

"Everybody could come here." Trudy's eyes lit. "I've been wanting to try this recipe I found for sea salt porterhouse steak."

Priscilla looked from tip to toe of Trudy's petite frame. "I thought you were on a diet."

"Oh, that was *last* week! I absolutely have to try this recipe, and Dan and I really shouldn't eat it all by ourselves."

Priscilla laughed. "If you say so. I'd love to come. I'm sure Gerald would too, as long as things are going all right with Ava."

Trudy's smile wilted. "Have you heard anything else about how she's doing?"

"Gerald was at work, so he couldn't really talk long. Besides, he probably hasn't heard anything new yet. You know how long hospitals and doctors and insurance companies take."

"Yeah. I'll be sure to pray for them. So what about tonight?" Trudy perked up again. "Do you want to get together tonight?"

Priscilla blinked at her. "Tonight? Can you have a meal like that ready by tonight? It's already midafternoon. We don't have to have anything fancy, you know. We don't even have to have a meal, if you don't want to. We could get together after dinner."

"Well, fine," Trudy huffed. "We could pick up Chinese."

"All right. Let me see if I can get Gail and Gerald to come."

Priscilla sighed. This had already become more complicated than she had planned, and it could all end up being nothing to worry about. Gerald had advised her to let Joan take care of her own business, but surely he realized now that there was at least some cause for concern. She'd just get everyone together and talk.

"I just wanted everybody to know," Priscilla said after she had told them all over dinner what Gerald had discovered about Calvin. "And, please, don't misunderstand me. I'm not saying he can't have reformed after he was in jail. Many people do. There are just some things that don't add up now, and I want us all to keep our eyes open in case he's got something going on."

"Like what?" Gail said, her gray eyes narrowed. Priscilla had expected her to be reluctant to interfere in Joan's personal business.

"Like how he makes a living in the first place," Priscilla said. "I saw some of the stuff he imports. It's interesting because it all comes from interesting places and is made by native craftsmen, but it's not that valuable. Besides that, he goes himself to pick it all up. That means days of travel each way on his yacht. That can't be very efficient or very economical."

Gail crossed her arms. "You said he sold a house on the beach and a car and whatever else so he could live on the boat. Maybe he has plenty of money from that. And maybe he just enjoys making the trips. A house on the beach? In California? You're not talking about a shack in Arkansas."

"That's possible," Trudy's husband said, glancing over at Gerald. "What I want to know is how dangerous it is for us or anyone to be snooping around someone who might be a drug smuggler."

Gerald's expression was grim. "It's no game, Dan. I don't want anybody doing anything stupid. Don't get in his way. Don't ask any obvious questions. Don't be alone with him."

"Joan's alone with him!" Trudy said.

"Not all the time," Priscilla said. "He's been to dinner at her house. I don't know for certain, but I'd be surprised if she hasn't been on his boat at least once. Otherwise, they're in public. At restaurants or at the pond or at Rayne's." She caught her breath.

"What is it?" Gerald asked.

Trudy frowned. "What about Rayne?"

"She's around him all the time," Priscilla said. "She has crates full of his stuff in her gallery. What if she looks too closely and sees something he doesn't want her to see?"

Trudy clutched her husband's arm. "Maybe we should tell the police."

"I don't know if there's anything we can actually tell them at this point," Gerald said. "We don't know anything. We just have to see what we can see."

"But Rayne," Priscilla said. "Should we warn her or something?"

Gail frowned. "That wouldn't be very fair. She's a business contact of his. What if she refuses to work with him anymore or ruins his reputation with her friends in the business and then all of this turns out to be nothing?"

"I wouldn't want to do that," Priscilla admitted. "I just don't feel right about all this." Before she could say anything else, her cell phone rang. Everyone looked at her questioningly as she dug it out of her purse. "It's Joan. Listen, I don't want to have to explain to her why we're all over here right now, okay?"

"We'll keep quiet," Gerald said.

Priscilla answered the phone. "Hi, Joan."

"Listen," Joan said, "I'm sorry I snapped at you today."

"No need to apologize. I should learn to mind my own business. I'm sorry I hurt your feelings."

"I just think you should get to know Calvin before you decide he's no good."

"I know," Priscilla said. "And, really, I don't want to be unfair to him."

"Thanks. That's all I'm asking of you. Of everybody. I, uh, want to ask a favor of you."

"Sure, if I can." Priscilla shrugged as everyone in the room looked questioningly at her. "What is it?"

"Well, I was talking to Calvin a little while ago, and he'd like you and Trudy and Gail to come to a party on his yacht."

"Just us three?"

Joan laughed. "No, of course not. I mean, it won't be a large party, but you're all welcome to bring whoever you want. He wants you to bring Gerald if you'd like. He likes Gerald. Trudy can bring Dan. Gail can bring Uncle Hugh if she'd like or anybody she wants to. Sort of an early Christmas party. He wants to get to know my family a little better."

"That sounds fun." Priscilla managed to sound more enthusiastic than she felt. "I'd love to come. Gerald's right here, let me ask him."

Gerald raised his eyebrows, and Priscilla extended Joan's invitation to him. "I can be there," he said.

"He said he could come," Priscilla told Joan.

"Great," Joan said. "Could you just tell Trudy and Gail about the party and see if they want to come? That'll save me a couple of phone calls. I have a lot to do before Wednesday."

"Wednesday?" Priscilla gasped, and everyone stared at her.

"Is that too soon?" Joan asked. "I know it's short notice, but with Christmas just two weeks from today, we didn't want to interfere with anything anyone else had planned. And Calvin is going to have to leave again on the twenty-sixth. Really, it's not anything fancy. Just come as you are. No need to bring anything. What do you say?"

"I guess it's okay with me. I'll ask the girls and get back to you."

"Ask her if she's going to take Sister aboard," Gerald whispered, his hazel eyes narrowed.

Priscilla gave him a puzzled glance. "Joan? Is Sister going aboard with you?"

Joan laughed. "I hadn't thought about it. Why?"

Priscilla's eyes widened. What was she supposed to say next? "Uh, I know Calvin said something about how he'd like having a dog on board. I didn't know if Sister was invited."

"Jake," Gerald mouthed. "Jake."

"I, uh, thought I might bring Jake with us too," Priscilla added, hoping she didn't sound too vague.

Gerald patted himself on the chest and then held his hand out about hip high. "Sammy," he mouthed. "Me and Sammy."

"And you know how Gerald is," Priscilla told Joan. "He doesn't like to leave Sammy behind."

"Uh, okay," Joan said. "They always have fun playing with Sister. I don't know why not. Calvin loves dogs. He'll be happy to have them."

"Okay, then. Wednesday it is. What time?"

"We thought about six. He wants to bring food in from a restaurant, so there's no need for anyone to bring anything."

"Are you sure it won't be too cold on the boat?"

"He says it's warmer than you'd think with the shrink wrap. And there's a nice space heater in the saloon. He's really eager to show everybody what a great host he is."

Priscilla gave Trudy an uncertain glance. "Is he?"

"He claims he is, and that he guarantees everybody will have a great time." Joan chuckled. "Anyway, we'll just eat and chat and get to know each other better. Will that work?"

"Six o'clock?" Priscilla asked Gerald, and he nodded. Trudy, Dan, and Gail nodded too. "Six is great," she told Joan. "I can't wait."

"I'll tell Calvin," Joan said. "And you'll see. There's more to him than you know."

"That's what I'm afraid of," Priscilla said to herself after she ended the call, and then she turned to Gerald. "What's up with the dogs? Are we really supposed to take Jake and Sammy to this party?"

"And maybe a friend of theirs too," Gerald said, a sly little smile on his face.

Priscilla frowned at him. "Just what are you up to?"

"Maybe nothing," Gerald admitted. "It depends on whether or not I can take out a loan from the office."

Everyone looked as puzzled as Priscilla felt.

"What's that supposed to mean?" she asked.

"I'll let you know on Wednesday."

CHAPTER SEVEN

The next morning, Priscilla set out on her own to do some
Christmas shopping. Rachel had recently moved to Boston,
and Priscilla wanted to get some nice things for her new apartment. She needed to get something for Gail's dad, Uncle Hugh,
who always said all he wanted for Christmas was peace and quiet
which, of course, wasn't all that helpful. And she still hadn't found
anything for Joan. All this business with Calvin had made her
want to find something especially meaningful for her favorite
cousin's gift. Something to let Joan know how much she loved and
cared for her.

After wandering around a few shops and finding nothing she
liked except a warm flannel shirt for Uncle Hugh, she found herself at Rayne's gallery. She didn't want to say anything to Rayne
about her concerns about Calvin, but she did want to look in on
her and get to know her a little better. Maybe if Calvin knew she
and Rayne were friends, he'd be less likely to try to take advantage
of her. If, she reminded herself, he was doing anything underhanded in the first place.

The jingle of the bell on the gallery door brought Rayne out of
the studio. This time instead of paint, her hands were covered with
streaks of wet clay.

"Hey!" she said with a smile. "Priscilla, how are you? Sorry I can't shake hands again. I seem to be always into something."

"Not a problem. I just wanted to have another look around. I still have some presents to buy, but I really don't know what I want. You have such an interesting mix of things in here, I thought I might see something perfect. That is," she added, "*if* I can afford it."

"If you find something you like, I'll make sure you can afford it."

"That's so nice of you, but I know you have to make a living too."

Rayne's eyes twinkled. "You've forgotten about my patron of the arts. He doesn't mind if I cut a friend a deal now and then."

"Donovan, right? Isn't that your husband's name?"

Rayne nodded as they passed the sculpture of the woman with the scene of a dilapidated Paris street in her head.

"He sounds like a nice guy," Priscilla said, slowing briefly to puzzle over the piece again. "Somebody who really looks after you. I'd like to meet him sometime."

"I wish you could. I thought you'd get to meet him tomorrow night, but he's not going to be able to come."

"Tomorrow?" Priscilla asked as they walked over to look at some gorgeous baroque-looking candle holders. "You mean at Calvin's party? I didn't know you were coming."

Rayne nodded, her loose curls nodding with her. "I think Calvin wants to get to know people around here. He seems like he wants to put down some roots, or at least see if this is somewhere he'd like to call home. From what he tells me, he's been just drifting around for the past few years, and he's getting a little tired of it."

"I can't fault his choice," Priscilla said, thinking how much she had grown to love the island in just the year and a half she'd been there. She smiled mischievously. "Can I see what you're working on?"

"Sure. Come on back."

Rayne led her into the studio. "It doesn't look like much yet, but—"

"What happened?" Priscilla asked, seeing the clumsily taped window near the back door.

Rayne winced. "Don't remind me. It makes me nervous."

"Did you have a break-in?" Priscilla moved closer to have a better look. "What did the police say?"

Rayne didn't meet her eyes. "I, uh, I didn't actually call them."

"Rayne! Why not?"

"Whoever it was didn't take anything that I can tell. I'm not even sure anyone got in. Maybe it wasn't even a break-in anyway. One time where I used to live, we had a really bad windstorm, and a shingle from the house across the street got torn off and flew into my front window. Broke it into a million pieces. Anyway, the guy is supposed to come fix it anytime now. I didn't want my insurance rates to go up by making a claim for such a little thing or reporting a break-in when I don't even know for sure there was one."

Priscilla looked around the studio. "But all the crates are gone."

"Yes. Thank goodness, all those pieces were picked up a couple of days ago. I don't know what I would have told Calvin if his imports had been stolen from my studio. I don't know how I would have ever repaid him for the loss."

"I'm glad you didn't have to worry about that," Priscilla said. "Does he have anything else for you?"

"He says he does, but the buyers aren't due in for a few days, so he hasn't moved any of it off his boat yet." Rayne gave her a knowing grin. "He seems to be a little bit distracted lately."

"Yeah."

Rayne's grin faded. "You don't think you really ought to worry about him with your cousin, do you? I mean, yeah, I don't know him all that well, but I don't know of any reason to suspect him of anything either. He made good on our deal with that first bunch of crates. And, especially this time of year, I can always use some extra money."

"I just think it's always good to keep your eyes open."

Rayne looked a little sheepish. "My husband tells me that all the time. He says I'm easy to take advantage of. Still, Calvin hasn't done anything underhanded."

Yet, Priscilla thought, but she smiled. "That's good. You just stay alert. With everybody. You haven't talked to that Peruvian lady again, have you?"

"She hasn't been back. Why? Do you think I should watch out for her too?"

"No more or less than you should for anyone else," Priscilla said. "I was just wondering about her. She seemed awfully eager to buy some of the things that were in those crates. You don't think she might have been trying to get in, do you?"

"Her?" Rayne shook her head, her dark eyes wide. "She doesn't seem like the type to do that. She seemed so refined. The type who'd use her money to get what she wanted if she was going to do something illegal, you know?"

"She could have used her money to hire someone to break in here," Priscilla said grimly.

Rayne bit her lip. "But I told you, nothing was taken. Nothing was disturbed. If for some reason someone did get in, he didn't find anything."

"You just be careful," Priscilla told her. "You're here alone a lot."

"Yeah," she said, grinning again. "But I could make somebody sorry if he tried to pull anything." She tugged at the chain around her neck and in the jumble of beads and other shiny, dangly objects were two slim canisters. "Pepper spray," she said. "And an air horn. Not that I've ever had any trouble, but Donovan insists. He says he'd worry too much about me all day if I didn't at least have these. And there's a panic button near the register and another one under the counter here in the studio."

"Sounds like your husband isn't taking any chances on losing you."

Rayne giggled girlishly. "He always takes good care of me."

"That's sweet." Priscilla reached over and gave her hand a squeeze. "I'm just sorry I can't meet him at the party tomorrow."

"Me too. But it ought to be fun anyway. Now, have you seen something you think might work for one of the presents you're looking for?"

"Well…" Priscilla led Rayne back out into the gallery and over to the baroque candle holders she had noticed when she came in. "I absolutely love these. They're a bit much for my little cottage, of course, but I have a friend in Seattle who'd love them in her house."

"Wonderful," Rayne said. "I'll give you my friends-and-family special discount."

Priscilla's mouth dropped open at the price she named. "Uh, wow. I'm sure that's a great deal for an original work of art, and they are lovely, but I hadn't planned on spending quite that much."

Rayne sighed. "I know. I really couldn't go any lower. I'm hardly breaking even as it is. People don't realize how much goes into a handcrafted piece unless they do that kind of work themselves. Then, of course, they're likely to just do it themselves."

"I'm sorry," Priscilla said. "They're really beautiful, and I'm sure they're worth every penny. I know what you mean about handwork too. If people knew how much it cost, besides the hours I put in, for the materials to make a quilt, they'd be shocked. That's why I give mine only to people who appreciate them."

"That's so true. I gave a niece of mine one of my original pieces, and she put it on her patio. The first time it got rained on, it was ruined." Rayne made a face and then laughed. "She's not getting another one anytime soon. Fortunately, though, there are collectors who are willing to pay what a piece is worth if they really like it."

"Like Calvin's buyers."

"Exactly. I even had another man come in asking about some South American art. That was after the last of what I had had been picked up, so I had to turn him down too. It's too bad, because he was extremely interested."

Priscilla frowned. How many people came looking for native South American art on Martha's Vineyard? She thought about it. "He didn't have a long ponytail, did he?"

"How'd you know that?"

"Tinted glasses? Tall? Thirty-something?"

Rayne looked at her warily. "Yeah. Do you know him?"

"He was at Mildred Pearson's museum the other day, asking her about South American exhibits and collections. I figured it was worth a guess that he might be the one asking you too. Really, I could count on one hand how many times I've heard any reference to anything even remotely related to South America since I've been here, and now that's all I seem to hear about."

"That *is* odd," Rayne said. "And I almost never have anything like that. Not until fairly recently. Between him and the lady from Peru, I feel like I've missed out on some good customers."

Just then the front bell jingled and in walked the ponytailed man himself.

"Well, hello," Priscilla said. "We were just talking about people who were interested in South American art. Did you ever find anything you were interested in? It's Justin, right?"

"Right." He shook her hand. "Justin Weir. And you're Priscilla."

"I am. How's the search going?"

He sighed. "Nowhere, I'm afraid. But that's why I came back here."

Rayne looked annoyed at his hopeful smile. "As I told you already, everything I had here that was from South America was already sold. It's not even here anymore. I'm sorry."

"Oh, I understand that. I don't mean to be a nuisance, but I thought you could put me in touch with the importer. I thought maybe he could make some suggestions on where I might find what I'm looking for."

"I'm sorry," Rayne said coolly, "but he doesn't usually sell to the public."

"I realize that, but I was hoping you could give me his name and number. I'd make sure to more than make up for any commission you'd lose on a sale."

"That's not it at all," she assured him. "He simply prefers to sell through galleries. I'm sorry."

"You know," Justin said with a smile, "I'm wondering if he might not be a friend of mine. Fiftyish, kinda stocky, real friendly. Is that your guy?"

"What's your friend's name?" Priscilla asked.

"Greg Mallory. Is he the one?"

"No," Rayne said. "That's not him. I'm sorry. But if you'd like to leave your name and number, I'd be happy to let you know if we get in anything from South or Central America. Anything substantial, as you mentioned."

"Sure thing."

He gave her a sleek business card with nothing on it but his name and telephone number. She put it in the pocket of the smock she was wearing.

"I'm sorry it's not Greg," Justin said. "I haven't seen him in a while. I'd like to do some catching up with him. Anyhow, sorry to have bothered you again. You give me a call if you get something in like we talked about."

Rayne patted her pocket. "I've got your card."

"You let me know now, okay?"

"Sure. If anything becomes available, I'll give you a call."

He nodded. "Merry Christmas, ladies."

Priscilla looked at Rayne once he was gone. "I didn't recognize the name of the guy he's looking for, but the description sure fit Calvin Gallico."

"That description could fit a lot of guys," Rayne said, but she didn't look at all comfortable with the thought. "And I certainly don't know anyone called Greg Mallory."

"Well, don't worry about it," Priscilla told her, feeling none too comfortable herself. "I'm sorry you missed out on another customer. Maybe you can get Calvin to bring in some things that aren't already sold. Something you could keep in your shop to sell to this kind of buyer."

"Maybe." Rayne smiled. "Maybe he and I can talk about it at the party tomorrow night. For now, I'd better get back to work before my clay turns into a lump of solid rock."

"Sounds good. See you tomorrow." Priscilla put her hand on the doorknob then turned back. "Don't hesitate to use that pepper spray if you need it."

"You'll hear the sneezing all the way over at your lighthouse," she said with a wink and a wry grin.

Wednesday night was almost pleasant for the time of year, and the stars were bright in the clear, moonless sky. Priscilla had hoped that Gerald would pick her up for the party, but he told her he would be coming straight from work, so she ended up riding with Trudy instead. Dan was in the front seat with her, and Priscilla got in the back with Gail. She put Jake in the middle.

"Is this thing with the dogs what I think it is?" Trudy asked.

"If you're thinking what I'm thinking," Priscilla told her. "I guess Gerald thinks it'll be a little less obvious with Jake around. Sammy and Sister too."

Gail rolled her eyes. "I suppose it's a good way to make sure we're all safe."

Dan frowned at her. "All of you just keep your eyes open. I don't think this guy would dare do anything with so many people aboard, but you never know."

"Don't go in there acting suspicious either," Priscilla told them. "If Gerald has some kind of plan, it won't do anybody any good if Calvin is tipped off ahead of time."

"What is the plan?" Trudy demanded. "You haven't told us anything."

"Because I don't know anything. Just keep your eyes open, like Dan said, and follow Gerald's lead."

Before long, they reached the private dock where the *Barrett* was moored. She was sleek and white, maybe a hundred feet long and twenty wide, and filled with light from the cabin windows that made the heavy-duty plastic covering glow. Calvin was leaning through the zippered opening, waving at them.

"Hey! You made it." He laughed. "And the doggie too. Well, he'll have company. Come on board."

"This is nice," Gail said as they stepped onto the teak deck.

"Thanks," Calvin said, beaming at her. "She's not much, but I call her home."

Dan glanced at Priscilla, and she knew exactly what he was thinking. This "not much" had to be worth a million or more.

"Thanks for having us," Priscilla said, tightening her hold on Jake's leash. "I think he smells something tasty."

"He's a smart dog."

Calvin led them to the saloon, a large room with a long, cream-colored sofa and matching chairs. A luscious display of hors d'oeuvres was spread out on the square teak coffee table. Rayne and Joan and another couple were standing nearby, chatting. Gerald was there too, and so were Sammy and a black-and-white springer spaniel Priscilla had never seen before.

"Have you met, Camilla?" Rayne asked

Priscilla noticed that Rayne was cuddling a little fawn-colored Chihuahua on the sofa next to her.

"Oh, how cute!" Trudy said.

"Well, Calvin told me the party was canine friendly, so I just had to bring her."

"Pleased to meet you, Camilla," Priscilla said, then she looked around. "I guess a few more introductions are in order."

"This is Roger and Carol Graham, who rent me this dock," Calvin said, indicating a couple in their sixties. "They live just up the hill, so I thought I'd have them over for dinner too. I think you all know everybody else."

"Except for Robbie here," Gerald said, and he brought the spaniel over to Priscilla. "I'm looking after him for a friend, and I couldn't very well leave him at home if Sammy was going to a party."

"Of course not."

Joan looked hopefully at Priscilla. "I'm glad you could come. All of you. Isn't the *Barrett* beautiful?"

"Gorgeous," Priscilla assured her. "I can't wait to see the rest of it."

"Oh, I'll definitely have to show her off," Calvin said. "Stem to stern. But first, let's eat. We don't want everything getting cold."

Gerald patted the spaniel's head as Priscilla came close to him.

"Robbie definitely wants to have a look at everything," he said just loud enough for her to hear.

Priscilla returned a subtle nod. A Coast Guard drug-sniffing dog was the perfect guest for such an occasion.

CHAPTER EIGHT

A dining table was already set at one end of the saloon.
Priscilla shed her coat and gloves and moved closer to the
space heater to get a little warmer. Hot cider warmed her even
more.

"Now," Calvin said, "if you'll all make yourselves comfortable
at the table and help yourselves, I'll cut up one of these steaks for
the dogs. No reason they can't have a treat too, right?"

He stuck the serving fork into a piece of meat, but Gerald
stopped him.

"Actually, I don't like Sammy to have anything with that much
fat on it. How about this one?"

He picked one more toward the bottom of the pile, and, with
a grin, Calvin speared that one.

"I think you're right, Gerald." He put the steak on an extra
plate and began cutting it into bite-sized pieces. "Healthier for the
pups."

He put the pieces into some small dishes and set them on the
floor under the coffee table near the sofa.

"Come and get it, boys and girls."

After the dogs began to eat, he put the steak Gerald had rejected
on his own plate and then served the rest to each of his guests. They

had already helped themselves to salad, a delicious-looking potato casserole, and what Priscilla was sure was the best French bread she had ever tasted.

"I know a guy," was all Calvin would say when Trudy and Gail both tried to find out where the bread had come from.

"He's always got a surprise of some kind," Joan said, smiling at Calvin.

He chuckled. "Nah, it's no big secret. I bought it at a little bakery not far from Rayne's. I like it better than what the steak-house serves with their meals. It's great, isn't it?"

"I knew it tasted familiar." Rayne closed her eyes. "Mmmm. I'll have to get some to take home to Donovan one of these days."

"I'm sorry he couldn't come," Priscilla said. "Maybe you could bring him along with you to the lighthouse when you come see it."

"If I can. He's not much for historical things." Rayne grinned. "He says the only antique he's interested in is me."

Priscilla smiled at her self-deprecating humor, though she couldn't imagine anyone making a crack like that about someone as young-looking and attractive as Rayne.

Dinner was surprisingly pleasant. The only thing that spoiled it for Priscilla was her constant worrying over what Calvin was up to and what Gerald was planning to do about it. Calvin kept Joan close to his side throughout the evening, but he seemed eager to get to know all of his guests better and to show off the *Barrett* to anyone who was interested.

"Who'd like a tour?" he asked once they had moved to the other part of the saloon to relax with coffee. "I know you would, Gerald, being a seafaring man yourself."

"I'd like that a lot." Gerald stood up too. "What about you, Priscilla? Care to have a look?"

"That'd be great." She looked at the rest of the guests. "Anyone else?"

"We wouldn't miss it!" Trudy said, pulling Dan out of his seat. Then she turned to Gail. "Come on."

Joan smiled and took the hand Calvin offered her. "Sure. Why not?"

"Not me," Rayne said. "I'm too stuffed to move."

The Graham couple, having already seen the yacht, wanted to stay and enjoy their cider. Jake was asleep under the coffee table. Sister and Camilla were playing like a pair of puppies with a chew toy, but Sammy and Robbie had both gotten up when Gerald did, and now they followed him out of the room.

The *Barrett* was much more spacious than Priscilla had expected.

"It's bigger than I need," Calvin said as he showed them into a bedroom with a double bed, lots of built-in cabinets, and a huge flat-screen television, "but I got a deal from a guy who was tired of living on the water."

"I think we should have one of these," Trudy told Dan.

He nodded solemnly. "As soon as you get us a couple million dollars, I'm in."

"It is amazing," Priscilla said, keeping half an eye on Gerald and the dogs.

"Really," Gerald said.

Careful to keep out of Calvin's sight, he leaned down to pat Robbie between the shoulder blades, and the spaniel began sniffing around the room.

"Hold on there, boy," he said, grabbing the dog's collar, but still letting him go wherever he wanted. "I don't know what's gotten into him. He's generally very obedient."

Priscilla forced herself not to smile. Whichever of Gerald's Coast Guard buddies had loaned him the dog, it was the perfect plan. Even if Calvin figured out what Robbie was doing, he couldn't say anything without exposing his criminal activity.

"I was eating a ham sandwich earlier today," Calvin said with a chuckle. "Maybe he can still smell it."

"Maybe, though after that steak you gave all the dogs, I don't know why he'd be too interested in ham. I'll have to ask his owner if he usually does this."

"No problem," Calvin said, still with a bit of humor in his expression. "He can't hurt anything. Let him go wherever he wants." He put Joan's arm through his and then patted her hand. "I told you I didn't mind having dogs aboard."

Joan smiled up at him. "I think Sister's having a great time with Camilla."

"Come on," Calvin said, "I'll show you the rest."

He took them through two other bedrooms with full-sized beds, a bedroom with two twin beds, and four bathrooms. Space was at a premium, so everything was designed to be compact and hidden away, but it was still an impressive place. Everywhere they went, Robbie tugged at his collar and sniffed around, wagging his tail furiously.

Finally they reached the last bedroom. It was fitted with twin beds too, but every available bit of space was occupied by a number of boxes and crates.

"Sorry about this one. I don't really have a hold, so I keep my merchandise in here. The other twin room was full last week, but all of that went to Rayne's before it was picked up."

The minute they entered the room, Sammy began to sniff and look around, but she stayed obediently at Gerald's heel. Robbie started whining and tugging harder against Gerald's hold on him.

Calvin frowned. "What's he after?"

Gerald glanced at Priscilla out of the corner of his eye and then turned to Calvin, his eyebrows innocently raised. "I don't know. There's nothing...unusual in here, is there?"

"Man, I don't think so." Calvin shrugged. "If there is, I'd rather know about it now. If it's a rat or a cat or something, you'd better let him find it."

"If you say so."

Gerald let go of Robbie's collar, and the dog immediately sprang forward, sniffing around on the floor. Around the crates. There was a gleam in Gerald's eye that told Priscilla things were going just as he'd hoped. The dog was after something. He pawed frantically in the dark, narrow space between two of the crates and then turned back to Gerald in triumph, a thick-cut piece of ham in his mouth. A gulp later, the ham was gone, and Robbie came to sit at Gerald's feet, the thump of his tail the only sign left of his earlier excitement.

"Uh-oh." Calvin looked guiltily at Joan. "Now you're going to think I'm an awful housekeeper. I told you I had a ham sandwich earlier on. I was in here checking some of my inventory, and I dropped my plate. Everything went everywhere, but I thought I got it all cleared up. Looks like I missed some."

"You keep the place very nice," Joan assured him. "Anybody could have a spill."

"Yeah, true. But that's the great thing about dogs, isn't it, Gerald? They can sniff out anything, even if it's not in plain sight."

"Yeah," Gerald muttered, and he took hold of Robbie's collar again. "Come on."

Calvin showed them all over the rest of the boat, from stem to stern, inviting them to look at everything, telling them how soundly she was built. Finally, they ended up back in the lounge with the others. Besides the ham, Robbie hadn't found anything.

At the end of the evening, Trudy and Dan took Gail home. Priscilla and Jake went with Gerald.

"Well, that was a joke," Gerald said after they'd driven for a moment in silence.

"It was a great idea." Priscilla looked at the three dogs sitting in the back of Gerald's black SUV. "You don't think that ham would have put Robbie off the scent, do you?"

"Nah. The way it was described to me, if you or I smelled a stew made with meat and carrots and potatoes, we'd smell stew. A dog would smell meat and carrots and potatoes separately. So, yeah, Robbie obviously smelled the ham. Sammy did too. But Robbie would have smelled the drugs as well, and he would have gone after them. They just weren't there."

Priscilla looked out the window. The night looked colder and emptier than it had before. "He knew all along, didn't he?"

"Yeah. I guess the whole dog thing was a little obvious," he said.

"Maybe. Why did you switch out the steaks?" Priscilla turned to look at him again. "Was there something wrong with the one he wanted to give the dogs?"

"Clever me, right? I thought there might be something in whatever he offered the dogs. He was suspicious right away. I could see it in that smirk of his. I figured he'd made us as soon as you said we wanted to bring the dogs with us. So when he wanted to give them that piece of meat, I got him to pick another one. But when he ate the first one himself, I decided there wasn't anything in it. But that piece of ham." Gerald gritted his teeth. "He was toying with us. With me. He knew right off what kind of dog Robbie is, and he was rubbing the whole thing in my face."

"But if drugs *had* been in there earlier, wouldn't Robbie have been able to smell them still?"

"I'm not sure. I'll have to ask Ben over at the station. Robbie's his specialty. Either way, I'm sure they're not anywhere on the boat now. And he still had all those crates to deliver. Robbie didn't notice anything unusual about them at all."

They were silent again until they pulled up in front of Priscilla's cottage.

"Maybe he was just having a little laugh at our expense," Priscilla said, though she was by no means convinced. "Maybe he's not doing anything illegal at all."

Gerald just looked at her.

Priscilla's concern grew. Gerald had done a complete one-eighty since the day he'd told her Calvin might be the best thing that ever happened to Joan. She wondered if his feelings of frustration and helplessness over his family's dilemma were making him even more cautious in this situation for Priscilla's family. She sighed. "Well, if it's not drugs, what is it?"

"Maybe it's not the what but the where," Gerald said. "Maybe he was just smart enough to get them off the boat and out to Rayne's before he could be caught with them. Maybe we should take Robbie over to her studio and see what he comes up with."

"Oh, I didn't tell you. Rayne had a window broken the other day. She says nothing's missing and she's not even sure it was anything but the wind, but I think it's quite a coincidence."

"Nothing's missing?" Gerald asked. "Nothing was taken out of those crates Calvin brought over to her place?"

"Evidently not. She said all of those items had already been picked up by the buyers."

Gerald nodded thoughtfully. "Could be somebody was interested in them and then left, seeing they were gone."

"Do you think Rayne's in any danger? She has pepper spray and an alarm, so she doesn't seem afraid to be there alone. But if someone's after whatever Calvin is bringing in, I'm worried about her."

"Me too," Gerald admitted. "But unless we have some kind of probable cause, we can't bring the authorities into it. Just keep on looking out for Rayne and for Joan too. Maybe, even if he is doing something bad, Calvin won't dare try anything here."

"And maybe I'm just seeing things where there's really nothing to see."

Gerald shook his head, his expression grim. "I'm not so sure. That boat of his is pretty darn impressive. He didn't get that by bumming around on the ocean and bringing back second-rate native art."

There seemed nothing to say to that, so she opened the door and got Jake out of the back seat. Gerald walked them up to the door.

"I don't want you to worry, okay? We'll figure this out."

She nodded. "Any news about Ava? How are Aggie and Nick?"

"Nothing much going on." He rubbed his forehead. "This is driving me crazy. There's got to be something I can do to help. I mean, to really help."

"I know." She squeezed his hand. "The important thing is that the baby gets the treatment she needs."

"Right. And we'll figure out everything else later."

He waited for her to unlock her door and then, with a parting grin, sprinted back to his SUV and drove away. As she stepped inside, her cell phone rang. It was Joan.

"Joan. What's up?"

"Hey, are you home now?"

"Just got in. Hang on a sec, let me get out of my things." Priscilla took off her coat, gloves, and hat and settled herself on the couch, wondering if she ought to get a fire started. "Okay, now tell me what's on your mind."

"Not much. I just was wondering, you know, if you had a good time and everything."

"It was a nice party," Priscilla said. "The food was delicious. That boat is really amazing too."

"Yeah, I know. But what about Calvin? What did you think?"

Priscilla hesitated. What could she say? "He was very friendly. It was really nice of him to show us all around. And the food was delicious."

"You said that already."

There was a moment of taut silence.

"Joan," Priscilla said finally.

"I know. You don't have to say it. You still don't like him."

"No," Priscilla admitted. "I can't say that I do. But that doesn't have anything to do with how you feel about him or whether or not you should spend time with him."

"No, it doesn't." Joan's voice was crisp. "I'm glad you realize that."

"Please don't be upset with me. I'm not trying to run your life or spoil your friendship with him or tell you you can't go out with anyone you choose."

For a moment, Joan didn't reply. Then she let out her breath. "I know. I just wish you would give him a chance. It wasn't very fair to do that to him tonight."

"Do what?"

"You were trying to catch him with something illegal. Don't think I don't know a drug dog when I see one. Gerald should have known better than to try something like that."

"It was nothing official," Priscilla protested. "We weren't trying to get anyone into trouble."

"It wasn't official because you don't have the slightest bit of evidence. Nothing that would make any judge issue a search warrant." Joan huffed. "It's just so unfair."

"Well, you're right about that," Priscilla said meekly. "I'm sorry."

There was another strained silence, and then Joan chuckled.

"That was bad of Calvin to lead you and Gerald all over the boat like that, but I can't say it didn't serve you both right. And *you* can't say he doesn't have a sense of humor."

Hilarious.

"No, I'm sure he got quite a giggle over it," Priscilla said. "But you ought to be happy we did it."

"Because?" Joan asked.

"Because now we all know he didn't have any drugs aboard."

"I never thought he did. Now will you all stop worrying so much about nothing?"

"I'll try," Priscilla said. "That's all I can promise. And I wouldn't be worried, *we* wouldn't be worried, if we didn't love you and care what happens to you."

"I know that." Joan's voice was a little warmer now. "And I appreciate it, but you don't need to be so silly about all this. There's nothing at all to be concerned about, so just relax."

"Are you home now?"

"Yeah. Sister and I stayed just long enough to help clean up and then we came home. She had fun with Rayne's little Chihuahua, but she's worn out now. Sound asleep."

"Good. Hey, what are you doing tomorrow?"

"Besides work?" Joan thought for a moment. "Just coming home and wrapping some Christmas presents."

"Do you have everything bought yet?"

"Not everything. I need to get something for Uncle Hugh and a couple of things for Gail."

"I still have a few things to get too," Priscilla said. "Want to shop?"

"That would be great. Just one ground rule."

"I know, I know. We won't talk about suspecting Calvin of anything."

That made Joan laugh. "Smart girl. I'll call you when I get off work. Want to have lunch first?"

"I'd love it. And, Joan?"

"Yes?"

"Thanks for not being too mad about the dog."

"Not too mad," Joan said affectionately. "Now have a good night's sleep, and I'll see you tomorrow."

Joan stopped by the cottage on her way home from work to pick up Priscilla and then drove them to the Little House Café.

"Too bad it's not taco night," Priscilla said, unable to keep her mouth from watering at the thought.

"I know, but last time I was here, they had chicken noodle soup that was just to die for. You should try it."

"I can smell it already. I think it would be just perfect on a day like today."

Priscilla ordered a ham-and-cheese muffuletta and a bowl of chicken noodle soup. Joan got the soup and a watercress sandwich. They did not talk about Calvin. Instead they discussed the art that was hanging from the walls of the restaurant, how Joan might discourage Sister from hiding her fuzzy bedroom slippers, and then, finally, where to go to find what they were looking for in the way of Christmas presents.

"What do you think you'll get for Uncle Hugh?" Priscilla asked. "He's always so hard to buy for."

"I know. It's like pulling teeth to get him to tell you what he wants. If he tells me 'peace and quiet' one more time..."

Priscilla couldn't help laughing. "I thought I was the only one he told that."

Joan rolled her eyes. "Good heavens, no. He's been telling me that ever since I was old enough to start buying presents on my own. Last year, he—"

She broke off, looking up, and Priscilla followed her gaze. Standing there at the side of their table, looking as exotic and stylish as before, was Alessandra Alvarez.

CHAPTER NINE

The Peruvian woman smiled when Priscilla and Joan noticed her, and her black eyes were intense. "I hope you don't mind my stopping by your table for a moment, Mrs. Grant. I trust you remember me from the art gallery the other day."

"Yes, of course I remember you." Priscilla glanced at Joan. "Is there something I can do for you?"

"This lady is a friend of yours?" Alessandra asked.

"My cousin," Priscilla said, unable to read her expression. "Why do you ask?"

"Forgive me," the woman said with a quick look at the door. "May I sit down for just a moment? I don't mean to interrupt your lunch, but there is something I must say to you."

Joan shrugged, and Priscilla indicated the chair between them.

Alessandra sat down and leaned forward, clearly not wishing to be overheard. "I have seen you with Mr. Mallory. Greg Mallory."

She was looking at Joan.

Joan shook her head. "I'm sorry, but I don't know—"

"Don't lie to me." Alessandra's whisper was fierce. "I have seen you with my own eyes."

"I tell you, I don't know anyone by that name. I'm sorry. I think you must have mistaken me for someone else."

"No, I have seen you." Alessandra turned to Priscilla. "She has not mentioned this man to you?"

Priscilla shook her head, but she had a strong suspicion who the woman was talking about. She had heard the name before even if Joan hadn't.

"He has a yacht in the harbor. The *Barrett*." Alessandra fixed her black eyes on Joan. "I have seen you there. Don't deny it."

"N-no."

Joan looked frightened now, and Priscilla put her hand on Alessandra's sleeve.

"We do know the man who lives on the *Barrett*, but that's not his name. At least, that's not the name he gave us."

"What name then?" Alessandra asked.

"Calvin Gallico. He's an importer. Neither of us has known him very long."

"I see." Alessandra's expression grew milder. "I mean neither of you any harm. I merely want to warn you. That man is not safe, whatever he calls himself. You would do well to get away from him and stay away from him."

"Why?" Joan set her jaw, her dark eyes snapping as if she were a little sparrow whose nest had been threatened. "What has he done?"

"That doesn't matter just now. And you must not tell him I spoke to you. I only wanted to warn you. I don't want you to be put in danger because of him."

Joan lifted her chin. "Just what do you know about him? And why should we believe you?"

A touch of a sardonic smile curled Alessandra's lips. "Ask him about Guadalupe."

"Who's Guadalupe?"

Alessandra's smile grew colder. "Tell him Guadalupe isn't a secret anymore."

"What does that mean?" Priscilla asked, and the woman shook her head.

"You had better not ask him anything. You had better not spend your time with him."

"Are you threatening us?"

"Not at all. I'm just trying to warn you. He hurts people. He will hurt you if you let him."

Joan pursed her lips, her dark eyes flashing fire. "You have no right—"

Alessandra lifted both hands in resignation and then got to her feet. "Merely a word to the wise."

With that, she walked away, not waiting for a response.

There were red patches on both of Joan's cheeks. "She's got a lot of nerve."

"Maybe you should listen to her," Priscilla suggested.

The red patches grew redder. "That was certainly convenient."

Priscilla frowned. "What do you mean?"

"Oh, don't pretend you don't know. She was all dramatic and scary, but she didn't really say anything specific that Calvin has done. Guadalupe? He's never mentioned a Guadalupe to me. Nice try though."

Priscilla's mouth dropped open. "You're not serious. You don't think I had anything to do with what she just said, do you?"

Joan didn't say anything.

"Joan! You're kidding, right?"

"You met her before," Joan said tautly. "She said as much. Is she the woman you were telling Calvin about when we had dinner at your house Sunday?"

"Yes."

"Exactly. And then she comes in here with that silly-sounding stuff about someone called Guadalupe and how dangerous Calvin is? And a fake name? And I'm supposed to believe it's *not* a setup?"

"Listen to me," Priscilla said, trying to keep her own temper in check. "*Look* at me. I am not lying to you. I am not in any way behind any of this. Yes, I met the woman at Rayne's for a few minutes. She was looking for some South American art. Peruvian, to be specific. She tried to find out who the importer was, but Rayne wouldn't give out the information. That's all I know about her. I did *not* put her up to this. I. Did. Not."

Joan's combative expression wilted. "Gerald didn't?"

"As far as I know, Gerald has never even met her. Besides, that name she called him, Greg Mallory, I heard it before from someone else."

"Someone else?"

Priscilla nodded. "A guy came into Mildred's museum. He was also looking for some South American stuff, and then he showed up at Rayne's asking for Greg Mallory."

"Maybe they both have Calvin mixed up with this Greg Mallory."

"I don't know. The description the man at Rayne's gave sure sounded like Calvin."

"Then that explains it." Joan sounded more like she was trying to convince herself than anyone else. "This Mallory guy looks something like Calvin, so they think he must *be* Calvin. I just need to tell Calvin about it, and he can straighten everything out for her."

"No! Joan, you really shouldn't—"

The waiter who had suddenly appeared at their table cleared his throat.

Priscilla forced a quick smile. "Oh, perfect timing. Doesn't that soup look great?"

"The chicken soup for you both," the young man said, giving them each a bowl. "And a watercress sandwich for you, ma'am, and one ham-and-cheese mufuletta. Is there anything else I can get for you?"

Priscilla's mufuletta was perfect, but somehow it didn't look all that enticing now. Still, she smiled. "I think we're good. Do you need anything, Joan?"

Joan shook her head, and the waiter went to check on a nearby table.

Priscilla put some crackers into her soup and then stirred it, making the fragrant steam rise in little clouds above the bowl. "At least we know it's hot enough."

"I am going to ask him about it," Joan said, stirring her own soup to cool it. "He has every right to defend himself. Who knows who that woman is or what she wants?" She put down her soup spoon, picked up half of her dainty-looking sandwich, and bit savagely into it.

Priscilla took a bite of her own sandwich. It should have been delicious, but she hardly tasted it. She couldn't let Joan do something foolish. Even though there wasn't really any evidence against Calvin, what Alessandra had said lined up with what Priscilla was already feeling.

"Are you sure you ought to do that?" she asked mildly.

"Yes."

"All right, but I'm going with you."

"Priscilla—"

"If there's nothing to what she said, then why not?"

"Because it's ridiculous. Calvin's been nothing but nice to me. Okay, so he gave Gerald a little bit of a runaround about the dog, but can you blame him? He's got to be tired of being suspected wherever he goes. And if he did change his name, who could blame him? Who wouldn't want a fresh start after what he's been through?"

"But he served time under the name he gave you," Priscilla said. "Under the name Calvin Gallico."

"Fine. Doesn't that prove he's telling me the truth about who he is?"

Priscilla took another bite of her sandwich, chewing it thoroughly as she thought of what to say. She didn't need to make Joan more protective of Calvin than she already was.

"I don't know what it means," she said finally, "but two people have asked for him as Greg Mallory. Two people have described him perfectly. Alessandra even saw him herself. Wouldn't she know if she had the wrong guy?"

Joan sighed. "I don't know. That's why I want to talk to him about it."

"I understand that. I don't know exactly what Alessandra thinks he might do, but she definitely thinks it's bad. That's why I want to go with you when you talk to him. If he can explain everything to you, then okay. Wouldn't you want me to know I don't have to worry about you?"

That made Joan smile just the tiniest bit. "That would be nice."

"And what would it hurt if I went along? If he's up to something, he probably won't do anything with a witness right there."

"I think it's ridiculous," Joan said. "But if it will put an end to all this espionage, I guess that's okay. Do you want me to call him and see if we can drop by the boat?"

"If you're ready, yeah. Let's do it."

"Fine." Joan fished her phone out of her purse and entered a number. "Hey," she said after a few seconds, "are you home?"

Priscilla couldn't hear anything but the low murmur of a man's voice in response.

"Oh, not much. Priscilla and I were out having lunch, and we plan to do a little bit of shopping afterward, but I was wondering if we could stop by for a minute."

There was a murmur in response.

"Just something we wanted to ask you. Is it okay if we head that way after we finish eating? Great. See you soon." She ended the call and then turned to Priscilla. "We're all set."

"Are you sure you want to do this?" Priscilla asked.

"If you are."

Joan began to eat her lunch again, and so did Priscilla. They didn't say much until they were finished and the waiter brought the check.

"Just give him a chance," Joan said while they were getting into their coats and gloves. "At least listen to what he has to say."

"That's fair enough. Uh, would it be okay if I let someone know what we're about to do?"

Joan snorted. "Gerald?"

"Don't you think that would be a good idea? Just in case, I mean."

Joan shook her head and wrapped her knitted scarf around her neck. "Sure. Why not? If it makes you feel better. I think it's ridiculous," she repeated, "but go ahead."

Priscilla grabbed her phone and called Gerald. He didn't sound too enthusiastic about her and Joan going to question Calvin.

"Just be careful," he said. "Call me when you get through talking to him. If I don't hear from you pretty soon, I'm coming over there, okay?"

"We'll try to make it quick," Priscilla promised him. "Whatever he's up to, we don't actually have any evidence, so there's no reason for him to do anything desperate. And Joan's right. He deserves a chance to explain, doesn't he?"

"I guess." Gerald was silent for a moment. "Anyway, you be careful. Don't antagonize him. And take anything he says with a grain of salt. And make sure to call me when you're through."

"Don't worry, I will."

Joan waited until Priscilla had ended the call before she pulled on her knitted cap and headed to the door. It didn't take long to drive to where the *Barrett* was docked. The weather had turned decidedly colder, but Calvin was out on the deck waiting for them.

"Come on in out of the cold," he said, bustling them into the saloon. "I've got hot coffee and cinnamon rolls."

"That sounds great," Joan said, smiling at him.

"Priscilla?" Calvin asked.

"Uh, the coffee, please. We just had lunch, so I'll have to pass on the cinnamon roll for now."

"Okay." Calvin poured the coffee and served Joan and himself each a heavily iced cinnamon roll. "Now what's going on? Did I do something wrong, Joanie?"

"Well, we were just talking." Joan glanced over at Priscilla, looking slightly annoyed. "We were having lunch when a woman came up to our table and told us we needed to be careful around you."

Calvin's bushy brows came together. "What? Why?"

"She said that you, well, that you hurt people." Joan looked at him pleadingly. "That's not true, is it?"

"Of course not," Calvin said. "Don't be ridiculous. I've had my share of trouble, like I told you." He gave Priscilla a sheepish half-smile. "I got myself into trouble with the law a few years ago, but I served time for it and never got in trouble again."

Priscilla nodded coolly. "We just wanted to know why you think this woman felt she needed to warn us about you. Especially Joan."

Calvin pressed his lips together. "She didn't happen to be a South American woman, did she? Tall? Well dressed? Very pretty?"

"Well, yes. She was. Obviously you know who it was."

"Yeah." Calvin ran one hand over his balding head. "What else did she say?"

"She mentioned Guadalupe."

Priscilla watched his eyes. There was just the tiniest bit of surprise in them before they narrowed.

"What did she say about Guadalupe?"

Joan looked at him warily. "She said Guadalupe isn't a secret anymore. Who is Guadalupe?"

Calvin looked into his coffee cup, silent for a moment, and then he lifted his eyes to Joan's. "Guadalupe was a big mistake. She's in the past, and I'd rather she stayed there."

"Who is she?" Joan asked again.

Calvin clutched his cup a little more tightly, and then he looked down. "She was the start of everything that went wrong with me. She was a Peruvian girl I met on the beach near our house in California. You saw Alessandra, the woman who warned you about me earlier. Think of her at about twenty years old wearing a white bikini and a big white sun hat and an ankle bracelet made of little white shells. That was Guadalupe when I first saw her. I had been going through some rocky times with my wife. You know how it is the first few years of marriage. It takes a lot of work, a lot of compromise, and I'll be honest with you, I was a stubborn idiot. I was tired of not being able to do what I wanted whenever I wanted, and I was about to tell Kelly that we were through, so, yeah, I was tempted with Guadalupe. I didn't try very hard to resist the temptation, either. I'm not proud of that. Then I found out that, besides a little fun, she was looking for someone she could go into business with."

"The drug business," Priscilla supplied.

"The drug business. Being on the beach like we were, especially in the secluded cove where the house was, it was a perfect setup. Her friends could bring the stuff up the coast from Peru and then disappear. Guadalupe and I could distribute it to dealers and everybody gets rich, right?"

Priscilla looked at him dubiously. "I thought you bought the beach house *after* you got out of prison. After you worked your way up in the import business."

He shrugged and took a sip of his coffee. "Different house, same lot. Kelly and I tore the first one down once I was back on my feet again after I did time, after I made good in imports, and then we built the new house. The new one is the one I sold to buy the boat."

"But what happened with Guadalupe?" Joan pressed.

"It was bad," Calvin admitted. "We got crossed with some really bad runners who wanted in on the deal Lupe and I had. It was so bad, I was afraid they were going to do something to Kelly, and I wanted out. I didn't like the kind of life I was living and the kind of things I was doing, so I told Lupe that was the last of it. I told her she could have everything, the whole operation, but that was the end of my part of it. After that…" He held up his hands, a gesture of helplessness. "After that, I didn't see her again. I thought I'd managed to get out just in time, when the police pulled me in. I hadn't gotten away with as much as I figured. So, I did five years, and you know the rest."

"But what about Guadalupe?" Joan asked. "What happened to her? And why isn't it a secret now?"

Calvin groaned and put his head in his hands. "I wish I could go back and do it all over."

CHAPTER TEN

I wish I could go back," Calvin said again, his voice heavy with regret. "I wish I could go back to when she was a pretty twenty-year-old walking down the beach. I wish I had let her just walk on by. I don't know. I tell myself she would have likely ended up the same way anyway, but I don't know that. Maybe if I had told her to go back to her family, to finish college and forget about the easy money and the party lifestyle, maybe it would have been different. I don't know."

"What happened to her?" Priscilla pressed.

"Evidently, the police took the information they got from me and used it to go after the runners who wanted in on our deal. In that business, if somebody's informing on you, you get rid of them, no questions asked. From what I heard, they thought Lupe was working with the cops, so they killed her and left her body as a warning. It wasn't pretty."

Joan's face was pale now. "But you weren't responsible for that."

"I don't know. Sometimes I think I wasn't, but if I hadn't told the police everything, maybe it wouldn't have come down the same way. They told me it would be easier for me if I cooperated, if I helped them get the really bad guys. I didn't think Lupe would get more than some time in prison. She was so young, I had no idea the runners would go after her."

There was the glimmer of a tear in Calvin's eye now, and Priscilla couldn't help feeling sorry for him. He wouldn't be the first to fall for the lure of easy money and end up with lifelong regrets.

"But who is Alessandra Alvarez in all this?" she asked after she had allowed him a minute to compose himself.

"Lupe was her sister. The police were supposed to keep my name out of this. I mean, about my giving information in the case. I don't know how she found out or what she wants now."

Joan looked bewildered. "But why was she asking for Greg Mallory? Who's he?"

"Me, I'm afraid. Anyway, that's the name I used when I was in the business. I wanted to keep from embarrassing my wife. It didn't actually help."

No one said anything for a moment. Priscilla took another drink of her coffee. It wasn't very warm anymore.

"What do you think Alessandra wants?" she asked eventually.

"I don't know." Calvin shook his head. "I really don't know. If she found out I was the one who got her sister killed, maybe she's after me. After all these years, I don't know how she could have found out. Maybe somebody we dealt with back then. Who knows?"

"Maybe she just wants to talk to someone who knew her sister at the end," Joan suggested.

"Could be. But I doubt it." His coffee cup clinked heavily against the table beside his chair. "She's been dogging me for months now. I thought I gave her the slip in Cuba this summer, but she's obviously caught up to me again."

"You don't think she's dangerous, do you?" Priscilla asked. "Shouldn't you tell the police about her?"

"I don't want to get into it." He pinched the bridge of his nose. "I don't think she'd kill me, but she sure seems bent on ruining me." He glanced at Joan. "Commercially and personally. She just follows me around and does her best to turn people against me." He looked up at the sky, shaking his head. "It's not like I don't understand. God forgive me, if I thought some jerk got my sister killed, I'd be after him too."

"You need to tell her to stop," Joan insisted. "Tell her what happened. I'm sure she'll understand. You didn't mean for her sister to be hurt."

"I don't think that matters at this point," Calvin said, reaching over to pat her hand. "But it's good of you to be concerned about me. No, I'll just do what I always do and move along. I don't want to have to talk to her at all."

Joan's face fell. "Oh."

Priscilla had to really bite her tongue to keep from telling Calvin he ought to follow his instinct and clear off. She couldn't do that to Joan. And maybe Joan was right. Didn't everybody deserve a second chance? That is, unless he was still a drug runner.

"She definitely knows where you are," Priscilla said. "I'm surprised she hasn't come to see you."

"Oh, that's not usually how she works." Calvin poured more coffee into his half-empty cup and offered some to Priscilla.

"No, thanks. I think I've had enough already."

"Anyway," Calvin went on as he topped off Joan's coffee, "she doesn't really have anything to say to me. I mean she pretty much blasted me the first time we met. They don't say Latin women are hot tempered for nothing."

Priscilla could see that in Alessandra. She was cool and elegant, certainly, but there was an intensity in her that might be indicative of a fiery temper.

"She'd rather trail after me everywhere and try to ruin things with my customers and any gallery owners I try to work with and, of course," Calvin added, "any personal relationships I might make."

"That's not fair," Joan said.

Calvin looked at her gratefully. "I don't want you to worry about her. I'm just going to stay clear of her and hope she doesn't try anything crazy. Besides smearing my reputation to everyone I come in contact with, she hasn't actually done anything."

"It's still not fair. And if she tries to tell me again how dangerous you are, I guess I'll just let her know I don't believe a word of it and that I can be pretty dangerous myself if I want to be."

Calvin beamed at Joan. "You're a peach. Did anybody ever tell you that? Because somebody sure should have by now."

Joan shook her head, laughing a little.

"So," he said, his usual cheerful self again, "anything else you'd like to know, Priscilla? I don't want you to think I'm keeping anything from you or your cousin here. I got tired of that about twenty years ago."

"No," Priscilla admitted. "I guess that covers everything. Thank you for telling us your side of it."

"I can't help it if Alessandra tells people all kinds of crazy things. She usually sounds pretty believable too. I wouldn't blame either of you if you believed her." He squeezed Joan's hand again. "I just don't want you to worry over any of this, okay?"

Joan nodded. "Okay."

"We'll do our best not to be taken in by anybody," Priscilla told him. *Not even you.*

"That's good. So what are you two up to now? Would you like to come back and have dinner with me later? It won't be much, just what I have on hand, but I can go out and get some things if you'd prefer."

"Actually, we were about to do some shopping and then I have plans," Priscilla said, glancing at her watch. "What do you think, Joan? If we're going to shop, we probably ought to get moving."

"Yes, I suppose we should." Joan got to her feet. "Call me later, Calvin?"

"You bet," he said, giving her a wink. "Priscilla, you are welcome to come back any time. You're always welcome."

He helped Joan into her coat while Priscilla wrapped herself up, and then they both followed him out the door that led to the deck.

"You two stay warm," he said, waving as they went back to Priscilla's SUV.

Priscilla didn't say anything when she drove away from the dock. She didn't know what to say. She still didn't trust the man, but was she being fair?

"Do you feel better about things now?" Joan asked her finally.

"I felt bad for him about Guadalupe. That has to be an awful thing to carry around all the time."

"I know. Especially when he was trying to start doing the right thing and help catch the bad guys."

Priscilla opened her mouth to answer and then snapped it shut again.

"What are you doing?" Joan asked when she pulled the SUV over behind a parked truck.

"Don't make it obvious, but look over there." Priscilla nodded toward the bait shop. "Under the awning."

Joan squinted that way. "That's Gerald, isn't it?"

"Yeah."

He wasn't in uniform, which was strange for this time of day, but even stranger was seeing who he was talking to.

Joan gasped softly. "That's her. That's Alessandra Alvarez."

"I know. Be still."

They watched and waited. Gerald and Alessandra were in the middle of an intense conversation. More than once they looked back toward the dock Priscilla and Joan had just left. Toward the *Barrett*. After a few minutes the Peruvian woman strode out into the bright winter sunlight and down the street. Gerald waited a few seconds longer and then disappeared into the shadows around the back.

Priscilla exhaled, just then realizing she'd been holding her breath. "Okay."

"What was that about?" Joan demanded. "Are you sure this isn't just a plan you two made to get me to suspect Calvin of something?"

"What are you talking about?"

"What were *they* talking about?" Joan's mouth was taut. "Why would Gerald be talking to her if it didn't have something to do with Calvin?"

"I don't know." Priscilla thought for a minute. "I guess it would have something to do with Calvin, but that doesn't mean we set it up. Don't be silly. Gerald's in the Coast Guard. It's his job to talk to people who might know about criminal activity."

"Then why isn't he in uniform?"

"I don't know. I just know that I didn't have anything to do with this, okay? If I did, I wouldn't have made sure to point them out to you, would I? I'm trying to find out the truth, not make it up."

Joan didn't say anything.

"Look," Priscilla said. "I'll ask Gerald about it. He'll tell me what's going on, and I'll let you know."

Still Joan was silent.

Priscilla took her hand. "I'm on your side."

Joan smiled at that, gave Priscilla's hand a squeeze, and then released it. "Okay. I'm not going to worry about any of this right now. We have shopping to do."

Priscilla sent a quick text to Gerald, letting him know they'd finished up and that they were fine and headed for shopping, and that she'd call him later when they could talk.

They had a good time, even though they window-shopped more than anything else. Each of them bought a few small things but left without the major items they had come to buy in the first place.

"I still don't have anything good for Rachel's new apartment," Priscilla said when they got back into the SUV with their purchases.

"What's the problem?" Joan asked. "There ought to be tons of stuff you could get for her."

"The problem is she already has most everything she needs, and it's all exactly what she wants. I'm afraid if I buy something for her that she doesn't like, she'll feel like she has to put it in her apartment anyway. And she'll never tell me how I ruined her home and her whole life until she's in therapy years later."

Joan snickered. "Give her something for the kitchen then. Something she can use and eventually wear out. Or get her a really good vacuum cleaner."

"All her kitchen stuff is new. All perfectly coordinated and not a dish towel out of place. And I gave her one of those automatic vacuum cleaners last year. I'm sure it's still running around cleaning up everything as usual."

Joan sighed. "I could use one of those."

"Couldn't we all. I'll just have to keep thinking."

Joan didn't mention Gerald again until they got to Joan's cottage.

"Could you just ask Gerald what he and Alessandra talked about?" Joan said before she opened the SUV door to get out. "If it's only business, then I guess that's what he has to do."

"I'll ask him. Just don't worry about it. You'd want to know if Calvin really is up to something, wouldn't you?"

Joan bit her lip, but then she nodded.

"All right then. Don't worry. Just pray that God will show us all the truth. Nobody wants anything but that, right?"

"Right." Joan got out with her packages and then leaned back into the door. "I had a good time."

With a smile and a wave, she hurried into her house.

Priscilla took her time driving home. She had to think. It made sense that Alessandra would want to make law enforcement suspicious of Calvin anywhere he went, if only to make it harder for him to carry out his business, legal or not. But why had Gerald met with her there? And why hadn't he been in uniform?

She called him up as promised after she brought her packages inside and took Jake for a quick walk.

"Hey," Gerald said. "What's up? What happened with Calvin? Is everything okay?"

"Yeah." She told him everything Calvin had told her and Joan about his drug-dealing days and about Guadalupe. "He seemed pretty torn up about her still. I guess that would be natural for anybody, even if it's technically not his fault."

"Yeah, I suppose. Did he say anything else?"

"Not much. I don't know what to make of him yet, but he sure seemed to have an explanation for everything we asked about. What do you think we should do now?"

"Let me do some checking, okay? I don't remember any mention of anyone called Guadalupe in the information I got on him. That doesn't mean it's not there somewhere, but I'd like to verify it all the same. For now, why don't you leave things where they are? Maybe he's telling the truth, and all the drug stuff is behind him now."

"But what about everything we were wondering about him when we talked before—"

"When we talked before, he hadn't told you about what happened to Guadalupe. Something like that can really get to a guy, you know? Let me do some more checking on him, okay?" he repeated. "I'll see what else I can dig up. Maybe there's nothing else that needs to be done."

She didn't quite know what to say. "Uh, okay. But you'll let me know what you find out, right?"

"If I find out anything. So how'd the shopping go? Did you get everything on your list?"

Obviously he didn't want to talk about Calvin anymore.

"It was fine," Priscilla said. "What are you doing?"

"Oh, just working as usual."

Out of uniform? That wasn't usual.

"Have you been busy?" she asked. "I'd think it's pretty quiet around the island this time of year."

"Oh, yeah. Not much going on. Pretty much staying in the station waiting for the end of my shift."

She almost told him she had seen him talking to Alessandra, but then she didn't. Maybe he couldn't talk about that at the station. Maybe he had stepped out for a break or something, and took advantage of the opportunity to continue their private investigation of Calvin Gallico.

"Have Aggie and Nick gotten any news yet about what Ava's treatment will cost them?"

He growled low in his throat. "It's ridiculous. Every time they try to nail down a total, they get the runaround. It's this and then it's that and then it's 'We can't tell you that until after it's done.' Who does that besides health care providers? You don't go into a restaurant and eat and then they tell you what it costs. Why should finding out the cost of medical care be so hard?"

"I know," Priscilla said. "I'm sorry. Still praying everything will get straightened out soon."

"Thanks for that." There was a sudden determination in his voice. "I'll figure out something. I'm not going to let Aggie and Nick go broke, and I'm not going to let Ava have anything but the very best care. I don't care what it takes."

She believed him. But just how far would he go?

"So, nothing exciting going on at the station?" she asked, making her voice as cheerful and breezy as she could. "Nothing new?"

"Nah, just routine stuff. Did you find anything particularly interesting while you and Joan were out?"

Yes. You talking to Alessandra Alvarez.

"Oh, we bought a few things," she said aloud. "Still a few more to get. You know how it is."

"Yeah, sure." Gerald's voice seemed just a little bit too hearty. "You two should just enjoy the season and not worry about things that might not even actually be a problem, okay?"

"Okay. And you'll let me know what else you find out about Calvin and Guadalupe?"

"Yeah, sure. As soon as I get around to it."

"Gerald…"

"Uh, I'd better get back to work. I really shouldn't be talking while I'm on duty. I'll call you soon."

He clicked off before she could say anything else.

She sat there on her couch with Jake happily panting beside her, wondering what to make of the conversation she'd just had. What had Alessandra said to him? And why did he seem so different now? She put her arm around Jake and pulled him closer so she could rest her cheek on top of his head.

"Maybe I'm just making a big deal about nothing," she told him.

Nothing Gerald had said was unreasonable. He was going to see what he could find out about Guadalupe in the records. He wanted Priscilla to be careful. That was a given whenever she tried to investigate something suspicious. He wouldn't be Gerald if he didn't try to protect everybody. Still, something about this just didn't feel right. Like the whole situation with Calvin, she just had this feeling, and it wasn't a good one.

She did a little bit of tidying around the house and then sat down to work on a quilt she had started a few months ago. It was all hand appliqué, a slow process that gave her plenty of time to think. She had planned on taking her time working on it, expecting to give it to Joan for her birthday in the spring, but now she thought she ought to get it done in time for Christmas. She hadn't found anything really special to give her cousin, something that would let her know how much she was loved and appreciated and that she was not alone in the world. All the blocks were done and sewn together, the borders had been added, but she still had to layer the top, batting, and backing, quilt the whole thing, and then bind the edges. Just thinking of all that still needed to be done made her tired. She didn't know how she'd finish in time, especially with everything she still had to do for Christmas and doing what she could to help Rachel get settled in her new place, but she was going to try. And she was going to find out what was going on with Calvin Gallico, no matter what Gerald said.

CHAPTER ELEVEN

The next day while she worked on Joan's quilt, Priscilla watched her favorite Christmas movies, *It's a Wonderful Life, A Christmas Carol,* and the original version of *How the Grinch Stole Christmas.* All of them were sweet reminders of Christmases past, but as always, they also made her think of how she lived her life. Was she living it to the fullest, knowing that everything she did affected the people she came in contact with? Was she lightening or increasing the burdens of those around her? Was her heart two sizes too small?

As the last of the credits rolled, she put the last stitch into the last block and then turned it over to tie a knot. She couldn't help thinking of Calvin again. He admitted he had done wrong. He had tried to do what he could to turn his life around. He had seen all too clearly the damage he had done. In his situation, wouldn't she have wanted a second chance? What if it had been Rachel who had made a wrong turn and only then realized how hard it was to get out?

Calvin and Joan were still weighing on her mind early the next morning as she was looking over the exhibits in the lighthouse, preparing for another tour. Actually, she couldn't really call it a tour. She didn't have many of those during the off season, but a man and his wife were coming in from Boston to have a look at the place, take photos, and possibly write a feature for their history blog. She was pretty flattered.

She had just returned to the cottage and made herself a hot cup of coffee when her phone rang. She was surprised to see *Aggie Hendricks* on the display.

"Aggie," she said when she answered. "How are you this morning?"

"Oh, hanging in there, you know." She sounded a little bit tired, but otherwise steady enough.

"How's the baby?"

"She's a little trouper." There was a smile in Aggie's voice, and then she sighed. "I just want to get her through this and then let her be a little girl again."

"I know," Priscilla said. "I'm glad the doctors feel they can take care of everything now so it won't be an ongoing problem she'll have to live with."

"Yeah, that's what we're hoping for. Thank God. And thank you and your cousin for all the great food. It's so much easier to deal with Ava's treatment when I don't have to worry about cooking and shopping and all that on top of it."

"You're welcome. We were happy to do it."

"Between you and the ladies at the church, we're eating like kings."

Priscilla chuckled. "Good. That's the way it should be."

"We're grateful, but I didn't call to talk about food."

"What can I do for you?" Priscilla asked, making herself comfortable on the couch with her coffee.

"Well...it's about Dad."

"What's going on?"

Aggie let out a slow breath. "I don't know. He won't tell me anything. He says he doesn't want me to worry, but that only makes me worry more."

Priscilla couldn't help smiling. "That's just your dad. You should know that better than I do."

"Yeah," Aggie said, "but it's more than that. He's all worried about the money we need for the baby. I told him that's our problem, Nick's and mine, but he says he's Ava's grandpa and he gets to take care of her too. And us."

"I can see him saying that," Priscilla admitted. "He's just that kind of guy. A good guy. He's trying to look after everybody."

"I know, but I don't want him making it hard on himself just because we're in a bind. We made our own choices, and we have to figure out how to live with them."

"But if it makes him happy..."

"It's not a question of that," Aggie said. "If it was just all of us pulling together, I'd understand and I'd be grateful, but this feels different to me. I don't know, like he's desperate or something."

"What has he said?" Priscilla asked, remembering the sight of him fading into the shadows after his meeting with Alessandra Alvarez.

"That's the problem. When I ask him what's on his mind, he just smiles and tells me not to worry, that he's getting it all worked out. That's all he'll say. Do you know what's going on with him? Has he told you anything at all? About work or anything? I don't want him doing something dangerous just to make a few extra bucks."

"He hasn't mentioned anything like that to me," Priscilla said. "I know he's worried about Ava and about your finances. I know he wants to help, but he hasn't told me anything specific about what he plans to do."

Anything. That's what Gerald had said he would do to help his daughter and her child. Absolutely anything.

"Has he done something in particular that concerns you?" Priscilla asked.

"Not really." Aggie paused for a moment. "A couple of nights ago he was at our house, and we were going over some things we could do to save some money, looking at possible payment options we have with the doctors and the hospitals and everybody else. Right in the middle of that, he got a call. I thought he'd let it go to his voice mail since he's been so concerned about all this, but he said he had to take it. Then he went out on the front porch to talk. Priscilla, it was freezing out that night! And when he came back in, he didn't want to say who it was. 'Just a guy,' was all he'd say. 'Don't worry about it.' Am I getting worried over nothing?"

Priscilla wanted to tell her about Alessandra Alvarez and everything she was concerned about herself, but she didn't want to add to Aggie's worries.

"I don't know," she admitted, "but I know what it's like to be troubled about something and not get any answers, so I'll see if I can get him to tell me what's going on. Maybe we're both making something out of nothing. You know how your dad is. He's the kind of man who puts other people first. That's what's so great about him, right?"

Aggie laughed. "Right. I just don't want him putting himself in danger because of money. I told him we'd work it out, but I don't think that made any difference."

"He can be a little stubborn," Priscilla said. "Just once in a while."

Aggie sighed. "Well, thanks for talking to me. I feel a little better anyway."

"I'm sorry I couldn't be much help, but I'll try to talk to him. Whatever he has going on, I'm sure he thinks it's best for all of you."

"I know, but I don't want him putting himself in a bind."

"Let me see what I can find out," Priscilla said, "and try not to worry."

So I'm not the only one wondering about Gerald, Priscilla thought as she ended the call. What could that call from "just a guy" have been about? Or was that "guy" possibly Alessandra Alvarez? Priscilla frowned and took a sip of coffee. It was cold now, only half gone. She went back into the kitchen and poured some hot coffee into the cup.

Maybe she should just come right out and ask Gerald about Alessandra. She had told Joan she'd ask him about her, but when it had come down to it, she had lost her nerve. She knew he was a good man, but what might a good man do to keep his family out of trouble? To keep his loved ones from harm? Maybe she should just trust him to know what he was doing. Maybe she ought to let him tell her what he wanted to tell her when he was ready to tell it. Wasn't that what friends did?

Besides, what did she know? Not a whole lot. She knew Calvin had served time for drug dealing. She knew his wife had died of cancer. She knew Guadalupe had been killed about twenty years ago. She knew Alessandra was her sister.

Priscilla thought a little while longer as she packed an overnight bag for her trip to Boston to help Rachel decorate her new place for Christmas. What else did she know? Gerald's drug dog hadn't found any sign of drugs on the *Barrett*. Alessandra didn't seem to be doing much more than talking to people. Why? And who was that Justin Weir who had been looking for South American art? Maybe he didn't have anything to do with Calvin at all. Or Alessandra. But it seemed like a really monumental coincidence that he would come to Martha's Vineyard, of all places, to shop for something Calvin just happened to have on hand, the same thing Alessandra had asked for. Besides that, like Alessandra, he had also asked for Calvin by his drug-dealing alias, Greg Mallory. That was far too large a coincidence to be believed.

Maybe Justin Weir was the key to the whole puzzle. Either way, it wouldn't hurt to find out.

Priscilla decided to stop and get a few last-minute things before she and Jake headed out of town. It was still early in the day, and she'd have all evening and then all day tomorrow to visit with her daughter. She ended up buying Rachel some decadently luxurious sheets and pillowcases in the deep blue that matched her new bedroom. She also bought a bag of some of the peanut butter candy Rachel always loved. It was cheap and it was certainly not nutritious, but it reminded her of Christmases past when Rachel was still a little girl and Gary used to tease her, saying he was going to eat all her candy after she had gone to sleep, which, of course, he would never do.

Eventually, Priscilla found herself at Rayne's gallery. Rayne was up front rearranging some of her art pieces. Everything in the window had been removed and replaced with a gorgeous collection of Victorian Christmas ornaments and mechanical toys. It was lit with soft twinkling lights, almost like flickering candles, that gave the whole display a nostalgic, even dreamlike quality. Priscilla stood huddled in her coat and stared for several minutes, knowing there was a wistful smile on her lips.

"Aren't they great?" Rayne asked when Priscilla finally came inside, her dark eyes bright. "I got a deal from a guy whose mother recently passed away. She had collected all this stuff for years and years, but he just wanted to get rid of it."

"It's wonderful. It always amazes me how intricate some of these old toys were. They're works of art all by themselves."

Rayne nodded eagerly. "It's amazing too, how they've managed to stay in such good condition after so many years. That carousel is probably from the 1830s, and yet it still turns and plays music. And the horses go up and down."

"Wow. I won't even ask how much that's worth. I'm glad you got a good deal on it though. Someone will love to have it."

"I hope so," Rayne said. "So what are you doing out and about today? More shopping?"

"Just a little more, but I thought I'd come see how you're doing. You didn't have any more trouble, did you? No more broken windows?"

Rayne shook her head. "Nothing like that. It's been pretty quiet."

"No one looking for South American art?" Priscilla teased.

"Ugh." Rayne rolled her eyes. "That guy was in here again. Yesterday."

"Which guy?"

"The one with the ponytail. Justin whatever his name is. Weir."

"You're kidding," Priscilla said. "What did he want?"

"Same as usual. He asked if I had gotten anything South or Central American in. Then he asked me again about my importer. I told him that I had given Calvin his information, though I didn't mention him by name, and I said he would get back to Justin if he had anything for him."

"Justin didn't happen to ask for anyone by name again, did he?"

"No."

"He didn't grill you about someone called Greg Mallory again?"

Rayne shook her head. "He didn't stay long. He looked around the gallery and then came back into the studio to look at some of those little things I have, the dolls and some of the pottery. I knew already that he wasn't interested in any of that. I'm sure he just wanted to make sure there really wasn't anything else. I didn't tell him that Calvin still has some crates on his boat that he's going to bring here."

"He was in the studio?" Priscilla asked. "Justin?"

"Yeah. Why?"

"I don't know." Priscilla looked around the gallery, frowning, and then she nodded toward the studio. "Have you looked around back there? There's nothing missing? The door's locked?"

"I've been extra careful about keeping the back door locked ever since that window was broken," Rayne said as she strode into the studio.

Priscilla followed her, looking around. It looked about the same as the last time she'd seen it. A half-finished abstract painting dominated by purples, teals, and golds sat on an easel near the window.

"Ooh, pretty."

"Thanks," Rayne said. "I don't know how I managed it, but I smeared part of it and didn't notice until this morning." She showed Priscilla a corner of the canvas where the gold looked smudged rather than brushed over the teal. "I guess most people wouldn't notice with a piece like this, but I never put paint anywhere but exactly where I want it. Now, though, I can't decide whether I like it better this way. Sometimes the best art happens all by itself. I don't know what I'm going to do with the rest of it quite yet, but it's a start." She stepped away from the painting and towards the back door. "Anyway, the door is locked."

She twisted the knob, and it didn't move.

"That's good to know. I just think you ought to be extra careful right now. I'm not satisfied that there isn't something going on."

"Don't worry." Rayne patted her flannel shirt just below the first button. "I still have my pepper spray and my little air horn. Donovan isn't going to let me go anywhere without them."

"I'm glad to know that, but that won't help keep your things safe when you're not here."

"I guess not, but the way I look at it, they're only things. They can be replaced."

Priscilla nodded toward the front window filled with what she was certain were valuable and rare antiques. "Some of them not so easily."

"That's true. I just wish I had been able to get ahold of that collection a week or two earlier. Yes, it's all perfect for Christmas, but Christmas is almost here. I would have liked to have it all out for people to see before they already bought their large purchases."

"True, but the nice thing is that Christmas will be around next year." Priscilla admired the painting again. "I don't know what you're going to end up with here, but I love these colors together."

"You'll have to come back and see," Rayne said. "Come back anytime."

"I'll do that. Meanwhile, you keep your doors locked."

Priscilla tugged at the back door again as she said this and it swung open, letting in a swirl of cold air and snowflakes.

Rayne gasped as Priscilla pushed the door closed again. "What?"

Her forehead wrinkled, Priscilla tried to turn the doorknob. It wouldn't budge. "Still locked. Hmm."

"How can that be?" Rayne asked, trying it herself. "But it is."

Priscilla tried it one more time and then unlocked it and turned the knob. The bolt moved in and out just as it should have. Then she locked it again. Again the knob wouldn't move. The bolt wouldn't move.

"That's just weird," Rayne said. "How could it—"

"This." Priscilla peeled a strip of clear shipping tape from over the strike plate. "The door was locked, but the bolt couldn't slide into place. It pushes in just enough to keep the door closed, but if you give it a tug, it opens right up. Anybody could have come in and out anytime at all."

Rayne shook her head, bewildered.

"When did you last open this door?" Priscilla asked her.

"I don't know. Not today, I'm sure. Maybe yesterday? Yesterday morning."

"Was that before or after Justin Weir was in here?"

"Uh, before." Rayne thought for a moment. "Yeah, I'm sure he came in after lunch, and the last time I went out that door was about nine or so in the morning. I took the trash out to the dumpster at the end of the alley."

"Don't you think you ought to call the police now?" Priscilla asked. "It's obvious that someone was in here after hours. Or wants to be."

"But I don't think anything was taken." Rayne looked around the room, hugging her arms around herself. "Do you really think someone got in here?'

"I do. Have you checked your computer? Your cash drawer? All of your art pieces?"

Rayne shrugged. "I know the cash is all right. I count it every morning and every night. Everything is just the way I had left it before. The computer's fine. Nothing's been taken. I don't know what to tell you."

"You ought to tell the police. Or at least your husband."

"Oh, good heavens, no!" Rayne laughed. "Donny'd have a fit and then he'd tell the police and after that he'd camp out here every day guarding me and making me too nervous to work."

"Rayne, you really ought to—"

"Look, nothing was taken. What if I just get a new lock put on the door? With a deadbolt. That way nobody could pull that trick with the tape."

"But the police ought to know about it. There is no not-sinister reason for someone to have put that tape there."

There was a look of genuine fear in Rayne's eyes, but then she laughed again. "I don't think Mr. Weir is dangerous. Just persistent. He thinks I have the kind of art pieces he wants even though I've told him a dozen times that I don't. Collectors can be extremely single-minded and determined, especially if they think one of their rival collectors has a leg up on them."

"Rayne."

Priscilla glanced around the room and then tugged Rayne over to one of the paint spattered chairs near her worktable. She took the other one herself.

"Look, Rayne, I don't want to scare you. I didn't want to bring this up at all, but I'm worried about you now."

"Worried? But—"

"Several years ago, Calvin Gallico was involved with drug smugglers. He served time for it. He says he's clean now, that he's just a legitimate importer, but I'm afraid there's something going on. Something illegal. Something dangerous."

"But what does that have to do with me?" Rayne bit her lip. "I've never had anything to do with drugs. I wouldn't know anything about them."

"That doesn't matter. Somebody might *think* you do. It might be that Calvin is innocent too, but if someone thinks he's bringing in something worth a lot of money, if someone thinks he might have brought it here to your studio, that someone might not care whether you know about it or not."

Rayne merely sat there, wide eyed.

"Please tell the police about this," Priscilla told her. "If there's nothing to it, at least you'll know."

"But Calvin's been so nice. He's paid me a good commission just to run his sales through my shop."

"Don't you think that's a little strange?" Priscilla was still holding the piece of tape she had pulled off the doorjamb, careful to touch it as little as possible, but she held it out toward Rayne. "Don't you think it's strange that two people would come looking for South American art, two people who just happened to know the name Calvin used when he was dealing? It seems pretty obvious that Justin Weir either came to look around or was plan-ning to as soon as he got an opportunity. He can't have thought you wouldn't notice this tape for very long."

"But wouldn't he have taken it with him when he left?" Rayne asked. "I mean, after he sneaked in?"

"Hmmm, I hadn't thought about that. Yes, I guess he would have. So that means he hasn't been back here yet."

"You don't think he's still coming, do you?" There was a tremor in Rayne's voice.

"I don't know why he would have taped the door if he wasn't." Priscilla glanced quickly at her watch. She really needed to get going if she was going to get to Boston soon enough to make the trip worthwhile, but she didn't feel comfortable leaving Rayne to deal with this alone either. "You really should tell this to the police."

CHAPTER TWELVE

A few minutes later, Officer April Brown came into Rayne's gallery. She smiled when she saw Priscilla waiting for her along with Rayne herself.

"I can't say I'm surprised to find you in the middle of another mystery." She pushed a lock of brown hair behind her ear and then turned to Rayne. "Why don't you start by telling me what's been happening?"

With lots of stops and starts and looking over at Priscilla for encouragement, Rayne told April about her dealings with Calvin Gallico and about the inquiries Justin Weir had made.

"I guess I don't know who else could have taped the back door," she admitted. "I didn't have that many people in here yesterday or today. Not until Priscilla came in. I think Justin Weir is the only one who came back into the studio."

"Not Mr. Gallico?" April asked.

"Well, yeah, he did, come to think of it. He came in this morning. He said he still has some things on his yacht he wants to bring over here, but he's not sure when he'll be able to do it. He wanted to know when I was going to be in the studio. He thought with Christmas coming up that I might not be keeping regular hours."

"He couldn't have just texted you?" April asked. "Called you on the phone?"

Priscilla was wondering the same thing.

"I don't know," Rayne said. "He told me he was on his way to go see Joan Abernathy. Maybe he just stopped by. I don't know. I don't know why he'd want to break in here. If he was smuggling something, and I don't think he is, why would he smuggle it into my studio and then break in to get it back?"

"You've got a point," April said.

She certainly did.

"But that doesn't explain what Justin Weir is after," Priscilla reminded them both.

"I'll be dusting for prints," April said. "Do you still have that piece of tape you pulled off the door?"

Priscilla handed it to her. "I tried to touch it as little as possible, but there might not be anything on it anyway. I'd guess he was at least smart enough to wear gloves."

April took a plastic bag out of her pocket and held it open so Priscilla could drop the tape into it. "We'll check it anyway." She gave Priscilla a sly look. "After all the cases you've been in on, I'm sure we already have your prints down at the station, so you won't need to let us take yours in order for us to rule you out."

Priscilla shook her head. "I think you're good on that."

"Do you need mine?" Rayne asked.

"Let me see if there are any besides what Priscilla put on here," April said. "Then we'll know if we need to rule yours out."

"I don't think you touched the tape, did you?" Priscilla said.

"Uh, no," Rayne said. "I guess I didn't. This whole thing is freaking me out so much, I don't even know what I'm doing."

"Is there anything else either of you think I should know?" April asked. "And, Rayne, you're sure there's nothing missing. Nothing out of place?"

Rayne shook her head. "We looked around a little while we were waiting for you to come. I don't see that anything's been touched at all."

"All right." April got up from the wooden chair she'd been sitting on. "It would be a good idea if you would put a better lock on both of your doors. Deadbolts too, especially in the back. You might even want to consider a security system. They're fairly reasonable these days, and you have a lot of valuable things in here."

"I'll do that," Rayne assured her. "I'll do it right away."

April nodded. "Better now than after something's happened, right?"

Rayne checked the back door again after April dusted the knob for fingerprints then left. "This is making me really nervous. I don't know if I can work here by myself anymore."

"Maybe you should close up," Priscilla said. "Just for the holidays."

"I can't do that. Business is already slow because it's the off season. I can't cut that down to no sales at all."

"Then I hope you'll do what April said about the locks and the security system."

"Oh, don't you worry about that. I'm going to call somebody right now. I just hope Donovan doesn't hear about this. You don't think it'll get around the island, do you?"

"I know I won't say anything," Priscilla assured her. "I doubt anyone else would."

"That's good. And Donny won't mind it if I change the locks and stuff. He's been wanting me to do that and get a security system too." Rayne gave her an infectious little grin. "I'll tell him I'm doing it as a Christmas present. For him."

Priscilla relaxed a little. "I bet he'll think making sure you're protected is the best present ever."

Priscilla hurried home to pick up Jake and her overnight bag and was just getting into her SUV when she saw Gerald and Sammy walking toward them.

"Good morning," he said, and then he glanced at his watch. "Or I guess it's just getting into afternoon. Going somewhere?"

"Boston," she said. "Rachel's waiting for me, and I'm already running late. I've had an interesting morning."

"I thought that might have been your SUV with the police car in front of Rayne's."

Priscilla's eyebrows went up. "You saw that?"

"You know me. I don't miss much. What happened? Is she okay?"

"She's fine." Priscilla told him about the tape on the door and everything else she and Rayne had told April Brown. "I only wish

I could be there when that Justin Weir tries to get in again. I'd like to know exactly what's going on with him."

"I'm glad Rayne was smart enough to call the police and not just ignore the probability that someone meant to get into her place after she locked up. Maybe it was Weir, and maybe it was someone else. Whoever it was, she's not trained to deal with a situation like that." Gerald looked at Priscilla keenly. "And neither are you."

She clenched her jaw. "I know that."

She did know. She knew it was risky, but deep inside, despite her more rational instincts, she had wanted to sit waiting in the darkness after the gallery closed for the night, waiting to see who might come through that door and what he or she wanted. It was a crazy idea and, thinking about it now, she knew it was stupid and far too dangerous. Far too terrifying. She knew what had happened to Guadalupe because she had taken a treacherous situation too lightly.

"I know," she said, softening her tone. "I know these people probably do whatever they think they have to in order to get what they want. And I know you're just trying to make sure we're all safe."

Gerald's taut expression relaxed a little. "I do want everybody to be safe. You've done your part by reporting suspicious activity. Now let the professionals do the rest." He gave her a wry grin. "That's why we make the big bucks."

She knew that wasn't true. It took someone who really loved the service, one who truly wanted to serve the country and protect her citizens, to do what was expected for the pay it offered. Gerald was that kind of man.

"I guess if that was really true," she said, "you wouldn't be so worried about how to pay for Ava's treatment."

His expression turned a little grim. "I'm working it out."

That's what he had told Aggie too. Nothing more.

"I was wondering though…" She wasn't quite sure how to approach this. "We don't know for sure that it was Justin Weir who put that tape on Rayne's door. She said Calvin had been in the studio too. But it could have been someone else entirely, right?"

Gerald shrugged. "Sure. I guess so."

Priscilla steeled herself and then forged ahead. "I'm just wondering whether it could have been Alessandra Alvarez. You know her connection with Calvin. Could she have had a reason to get into the studio?"

"I don't know." Gerald's face was expressionless. "I suppose so."

"Did you ever check to see if there was anything about her sister Guadalupe in Calvin's record?"

Gerald didn't answer.

Priscilla waited a moment and then frowned. "Well, did you?"

"Yeah," Gerald said, his voice brusque.

Priscilla's frown deepened when he said nothing else. "And?"

"There's no mention of a girl at all, Guadalupe or otherwise. Just the reference about him doing time in California for dealing drugs. They used information they got from him to take down some of the bigger guys he was selling for. That much is true."

"But—"

"Look, I know you're worried about what's going on with Calvin and Joan, but I really wish you would just stay out of it. Let them mind their own business, whatever it is, let the police take care of what's going on at Rayne's, if there is actually anything, and let Calvin alone. He has every right to carry on his affairs without being harassed by anybody."

"Harassed?" Priscilla's mouth tightened. "Is that what you think I'm doing? Harassing people?"

"I didn't say that. I just think it would be good if you backed off a bit."

Tears burned behind Priscilla's eyes but she was not going to let them show. Did he really think she was harassing people? Had he thought that the entire time they'd been friends?

"All I'm trying to do is help," she said tightly.

"Don't get mad, okay?" He gave her a worried look. "I'm not trying to hurt your feelings. I want you to be safe. I just want you to stay out of trouble."

"But if there's not enough evidence to get the police involved, I can't stand by and let Joan get hurt."

"If there's not enough evidence to get them involved, maybe it's because there's nothing to worry about."

"I don't think you believe that. You were the one who brought the drug dog onto his boat."

"Yeah," Gerald said, "and I'm the one who didn't find anything either. Rayne said nothing was taken from her place, and she has all those valuable antiques in there. Joan just wants to enjoy having somebody to spend her time with. Why is that so bad?"

"Because I know something's wrong." Now a tear did slip down her cheek, and she dashed it away with the back of her hand, furious with herself. "I don't have anything really specific, just a few inconsistencies and a bad feeling. But I still know."

"Priscilla," he said gently, reaching for her hand, but she pulled away.

"I appreciate your help," she said coolly. "I'm sorry to have wasted your time."

"Don't be that way now. Come on. I know you're upset about all this, but until we know more—"

"No, it's all right. I know you have a lot to deal with right now besides my silly little problems."

"I never said any of this was silly."

She was hurting him now, and she didn't want that. She made her voice a little less taut.

"It's okay. I mean it. You're right about there not being any evidence. Maybe I've gotten too paranoid lately and see something suspicious wherever I look."

He grinned a little. "I've been that way ever since I joined the Coast Guard. I have to remind myself I'm not always on duty."

"Anyway, I'm serious. You have enough on your plate as it is with what's going on with your family. I'm sure the police will take care of anything that might actually come up with Calvin. It's their job after all."

"Okay." There was a touch of wariness in his voice, but he didn't argue with her. "Anyway, I guess I'd better get moving. I know you have to get to Rachel's, and I'm supposed to have dinner at Aggie's again. She got some more information from the insurance company, so we're going to look it over."

"I hope it's good news," Priscilla said. "And, please, let me know if there's anything I can do."

He was leaning down, scratching Sammy's ears, but he looked up into Priscilla's eyes. "The best thing you can do is not give me anything else to worry about by keeping out of harm's way."

"I hope you'll do the same thing," she said, and something foreboding tightened around her heart.

"It's my job to be in harm's way, remember? I'll talk to you soon. Come on, Sammy."

Priscilla opened her car door and stood watching them until they were out of sight. Then she got in the car and headed out. She wasn't going to do anything stupid, but that didn't mean she was going to quit trying to figure out what Calvin Gallico was up to. If Gerald wanted to have his little secrets, she could have hers too.

Priscilla came back from Boston late Saturday afternoon. Though Rachel's ultra-modern silver and blue theme wouldn't have been her first choice, Priscilla had to admit the apartment looked elegant once they were finished. On the way home, she couldn't resist stopping by Rayne's gallery to see what had happened overnight.

"Nothing," Rayne said with a sigh. "Officer Brown sent some-one over to tape the door the way it had been earlier, and then they sent me home. The officer staked out the place to see if anyone tried to come in, but nobody ever did. It was totally quiet."

"That's too bad," Priscilla said. "Whoever it was must have seen April's squad car here earlier in the day and knew something was up."

Gerald had noticed that April was at the gallery. Surely he didn't have anything to do with tipping off the potential burglar. She wasn't going to even think that.

"I guess so," Rayne said. "I wish whoever it is would just go away."

Priscilla looked at her for a moment. "Are you sure you haven't seen anything about Calvin that seems suspicious to you? Not any-thing at all?"

"Nothing. But after we talked I started thinking about South America and what people smuggle out of there. And Calvin hav-ing been involved with drug people, I don't know. It just makes me worry. I don't think he's involved, at least not what he's brought in here. It's all just pottery and things. I'd have noticed if there was anything else. But what if those people—Justin or Alessandra or whoever else there might be—what if they just think he's smug-gling something? Or what if they're after him because of what he did twenty years ago? What if they think *I* know something about it?"

"That's why I want you to be careful. Maybe you shouldn't work with Calvin anymore."

"You don't think I have to keep worrying about someone coming in, do you?" Rayne's dark eyes were anxious. "I got the locks changed and deadbolts put on." She showed Priscilla the new lock on the front door. It looked very sturdy. "The one on the back is just the same. And someone's coming to talk to me about installing a security system on Monday."

"That's good. You still need to be careful and make extra sure the doors are securely locked when you close up every night."

"Oh, believe me, Donny gave me that lecture yesterday. I won't forget."

"What else did the police tell you? Anything?"

Rayne shrugged. "She took Justin's phone number and said they would be getting in touch with him. There were no fingerprints except yours on the tape, so they don't have any actual evidence against him, but they'll ask some questions anyway. Other than that, there's not much they can do."

Priscilla groaned. "This is so frustrating. I wish I could just call Justin myself and ask him what's going on."

Rayne's eyes widened. "You wouldn't really."

"No," Priscilla said with a sigh. "Especially if the police have already contacted him about this. He'd definitely know something was up, and if he's the kind of bad guy we think he might be, it would be dangerous. I'd still like to know what he's looking for. You didn't ever tell him where Calvin is, did you?"

Rayne shook her head. "But he must know that's who I'm working with. It couldn't be too hard for him to watch the gallery until Calvin comes back and then follow him to his boat."

"True," Priscilla said, but her mind was suddenly racing. Maybe there was another way to find out about Justin Weir. "Just let me know if you see or hear anything else," she said as she hurriedly buttoned up her coat to go back out into the cold. "And be careful."

Looking puzzled, Rayne walked her back to the gallery door. "You make sure to take your own advice."

CHAPTER THIRTEEN

As soon as she got into her SUV, Priscilla dialed Joan's number.

"Hey, Joan. How are things going?"

"Good. How about you?"

Joan's voice was particularly chipper. Priscilla could guess why.

"I was just wondering what you were doing tonight," she said. "I was going to bake some sugar cookies. You know, the kind with the sparkly sugar decorations? I thought it would be more fun with somebody besides Jake."

Joan laughed. "That does sound like fun, and I'd love to, but I already have plans for tonight."

"Oh, really?" Priscilla was fairly sure she knew who was involved in those plans.

"Maybe you could call Trudy and Gail."

"I haven't tried them yet, because first I wanted to see if you already had plans. Maybe we can do it tomorrow or something. Are you going out with Calvin?"

"Actually, he's coming here for dinner." Joan's voice was cooler now. "It's just dinner, okay?"

"Sure. I guess. You don't need my permission."

"I was starting to wonder."

Priscilla winced at that. This wasn't going to be easy.

"Look, Joan, I need to ask a favor of you. Please don't be mad."

"Are you still trying to prove Calvin is a criminal?" Joan very definitely did not sound not mad.

"I'm trying to prove he's not!" Priscilla pressed her lips together, waiting a moment until she was calmer. "There is evidence that someone wanted to break into Rayne's studio last night. Nothing happened, and she's okay, but everything points toward Justin Weir being the guy making the attempt."

Joan said nothing.

"Justin is one of the two people who have asked about Calvin using the name Greg Mallory, the name Calvin used to use when he was in the drug business. Justin's been asking where Greg Mallory is and pressing to meet with him. If Calvin isn't involved in smuggling anymore, don't you think that's strange?"

"Maybe," Joan said, her voice tight.

"Don't you think Calvin ought to know what's going on with Justin?"

"Oh, no. You are not coming over here to accuse him of I don't know what."

"That's exactly it. You don't know what. I don't know what. But maybe Calvin does. He explained about what happened to Guadalupe." *Even though Gerald found no mention of her in Calvin's records.* "If Justin Weir thinks Calvin is involved in drugs somehow and Calvin is innocent, don't you think Calvin should know about it? Calvin informed on some dealers, and that's what got

Guadalupe killed. Maybe Justin is one of their guys, sent to make an example of him too."

"After twenty years?" Joan sounded more worried than skeptical.

"I don't know. Maybe. But shouldn't he know about it?"

"Didn't Rayne tell him Justin wanted to meet with him?"

Priscilla thought for a minute. "I think she was going to, but she didn't tell me specifically that she did. I suppose she has. But wouldn't you feel better if you knew why Justin was looking for him? And wouldn't you feel better knowing for sure that he knew Justin was trying to find him?"

"Maybe Justin is just what he says he is," Joan suggested. "Maybe he just wants to find some good South American art."

"Then why did he ask for Calvin under the name he used when he was dealing drugs?"

"How old did you say this guy looks?" Joan asked. "Thirty something?"

"Probably."

"Then how could he be a holdover from Calvin's drug days? What was he doing? Dealing at age ten?"

Priscilla hadn't thought of that before. "He could have been sent by somebody. Somebody who knew him back then and knew he trafficked in drugs and wanted to get in on the deal."

"So there's nobody else in the whole world after twenty years someone could get in touch with to sell drugs? Only Calvin? Really?"

Priscilla could easily imagine Joan standing with one hand on her hip, scowling in exasperation.

"That would be ridiculous," Priscilla said evenly. "Unless he was still involved in smuggling."

There was absolute silence on the other end of the line.

"Can you think of another reason?" Priscilla asked finally.

Still there was silence. Then she heard Joan exhale.

"All right, fine. Come over. Tell him about Justin. See what he says. You were so sure you knew he was a criminal the last time. And before that with that ridiculous dog. I'll tell him to expect you to be here when he gets here, but only for a few minutes."

"No, don't tell him that. Good heavens, that'll just give him a lot of time to make up a good story."

"I really ought to hang up on you right now," Joan said, "but you're right, I do want to know what's going on. The truth. And I guess he's the best one to ask."

"That's all I'm looking for, Joan. Really. I care about you too much to let something awful happen to you. If he can explain everything, maybe I won't worry about you so much with him."

"Maybe if you stopped looking for reasons to be suspicious of him, you wouldn't worry so much either." Joan's voice wasn't exactly warm now, but she didn't sound quite so angry either. "And I know you mean well."

"I do. It's just with everything I've heard about—"

"Let's not go over all that again, okay? He's coming at seven. You'd better be here a few minutes before that, and then, after you apologize to him, you can leave."

"I'll ask him about Justin and then leave you two in peace. I promise."

It seemed like seven o'clock would never arrive. Priscilla was twenty minutes early as it was and found Sister sound asleep in her crate. Joan was in the middle of putting on makeup and doing her hair. She was never much for getting dressed up, and to be honest, Priscilla loved seeing her excited about having someone special, loved seeing her feel like she was worth being pursued. Too bad the one pursuing her was as questionable a man as Calvin Gallico.

Priscilla helped Joan finish getting ready and then helped set the table and do a few last-minute things in the kitchen. Joan had cooked a divine-smelling roast with a vegetable casserole and roasted red potatoes. And in the refrigerator, looking like a work of art, was a frothy strawberry trifle. Calvin certainly would have nothing to complain about with the food, that is if he wasn't too offended by Priscilla's questions to stay long enough to eat it.

Dear Lord, she prayed silently, *please give me the right words to say, and let me listen without prejudice to what he has to say in response. You know his heart, not me. Help me see the truth and keep us safe.*

The doorbell rang on her amen, and she felt her heart beat a little faster. How she wished Gerald was here too, or at least that he knew she was here. But she hadn't told him anything. She had told Trudy. In case anything happened, she told herself, though, despite her fears, she couldn't really imagine it. The worst he would do is get mad and leave, right? And then Joan would be mad too, really mad, but that was all. That wasn't fatal, was it?

"Lord," she whispered as Joan opened the door, "keep us safe."

There was a quick rush of cold, wet-smelling air, and then Joan shut the door again. Calvin wore a heavy wool overcoat and his fedora and a striped scarf of knitted brown wool. His broad smile faltered a little when he saw Priscilla standing in the kitchen door.

"Well, Priscilla. I thought that looked like your SUV out front, but I didn't think Joanie and I'd have any company tonight." He took off his coat, hat, and scarf and left them on one of the chairs by the fire. "Er, good to see you."

"Don't worry, I'm not staying. I just had something to ask you about, so I twisted Joan's arm and made her let me come by for a minute."

She hoped her expression was unthreatening, maybe even a little apologetic but not accusing. She didn't need to make him any more wary than he was.

"Priscilla was good enough to give me a little help getting ready," Joan said, smoothing back the hair that turned under against the side of her neck.

Calvin looked her up and down with a comical raising of his heavy eyebrows. "You look like a million bucks, that's what I say. Not a penny less."

Joan turned a little pink and wouldn't look at Priscilla. "Why don't we all have a seat? Dinner's not quite ready yet, so we might as well let Priscilla say what she wants to say before she has to go."

Calvin looked at Joan and then briefly at Priscilla. "Uh, yeah, sure. Why not?"

They sat on the sofa with Joan in the middle.

"I know you two want to get to your dinner," Priscilla said, "so I'll get right to it. Please understand, Calvin, that I'm just trying to get some answers. I'm not accusing anyone of anything."

Calvin looked less than reassured. "Okay."

"Do you know someone named Justin Weir?"

Calvin shook his head.

"Well, he knows you," Priscilla said. "Or at least he knows *of* you."

"Who is he? What does he want?"

"I'm not sure," Priscilla admitted. "I just know he's been asking around town for someone who fits your description by the name of Greg Mallory."

"What? Why?"

"I thought maybe you'd know."

Calvin looked around as if he expected the man to pop out from behind the curtain or something. "What's he been saying?"

"He says he's looking for South American art and that Greg Mallory is an importer he knows. Why would he think that?"

"Look, I know what you're thinking, but I've been out of the drug business for twenty-something years." He pulled a handkerchief out of his pocket and mopped his face with it. "I'll take a polygraph test if you want me to. What's this guy look like?"

Priscilla described Justin, and Calvin shook his head.

"I can't remember anybody like that. Thirtysomething? Too young to be from my time dealing."

Priscilla said nothing for a minute or so, waiting for him to come up with a glib answer, but he didn't seem to have one this time.

"I just don't know," he said at last. "Weir. I don't know anyone named Weir. Maybe he is just looking for some good pieces from South America."

"Then why would he be looking for Greg Mallory and not Calvin Gallico?"

"I tell you I—" Calvin broke off. "No," he muttered under his breath. "No, no, no."

Joan grabbed his hand, her dark eyes full of worry. "What is it? What's wrong?"

"No," he said again, shaking his head. "No, it can't be."

"What?" Joan urged.

"There was a guy I knew, Max Moran. One of the big guys' lieutenants. He was the big guy's brother-in-law too. He had a boy named Justin. I don't know, ten, twelve years old. When Guadalupe was killed, the police tried to crack down on a lot of the people in the business. They used the information I gave them to bust a house in Fresno. Three or four guys were killed. Max was one of them. Justin...Justin's got to be the kid. There's no other way it fits. Max was crazy about him, always saying how smart he was in school. Going to be a doctor. Not going to be involved in dirty stuff like his father. Oh, man." Calvin blotted his face again. "Oh, man, oh, man, oh, man."

"But why would he be looking for you now?" Joan asked.

"Why wouldn't he?" Calvin snapped. "Come on, Joan, I got his dad killed."

"No, you didn't," she soothed. "He put himself in danger because he was a criminal. You did the right thing, trying to get out of that lifestyle."

"If you think he's dangerous, you ought to tell the police," Priscilla said. "He hasn't tried to contact you?"

"Just through Rayne." Calvin ran both hands through his thinning hair. "I didn't think anything of it. I have a lot of people who want to deal directly with me, but that's not my thing. I tell most of the art dealers I work with that it's because I don't want to be bothered with the red tape of retail sales." He squeezed Joan's hand a little more tightly. "But I also just don't want to meet a lot of people. I don't want to run into anybody from the old days, anybody who might have it in for me. Yeah, I'm square with the police and all that, but I'm always looking over my shoulder. I was stupid to think I could mess around in the drug business. There's a lot of money and a lot of power involved, and it's not so easy to get out once you're in."

"You have to tell the police," Joan said. "They'll arrest this guy. He can't just go around killing people."

"I don't have anything on him," Calvin told her. "He doesn't even have the same last name as the guy I knew. Maybe I'm totally wrong about who he is and what he wants." He squeezed his eyes shut. "But I'm not. I know I'm not. Man, I know I'm not."

"So he changed his name." Joan made him look at her. "There have to be some records from that. They would prove who he is. Then they'd have to make him leave you alone."

"No. He'd make up something they'd believe. There's nothing they could do to him anyway. He hasn't done anything but ask for an importer named Greg Mallory. They wouldn't be able to do anything to him until after he got to me."

"What will you do?" Priscilla asked. The man looked genuinely scared.

"I—" He took a deep breath, steadying himself. "I have people coming in Monday afternoon to pick up the last of the things I have on my boat. I'm supposed to take them over to Rayne's Monday morning. After that, I think I'd better get off the island for a while."

"Oh," Joan murmured.

"Don't worry, Joanie. It's just for a while. When this guy realizes I'm gone, he'll move on too. Then maybe I'll come right back here."

"But won't it be dangerous for you here until then? What if he finds you tonight or sometime tomorrow? Or even after you've gone to Rayne's?"

"Look, I don't mean any harm to anybody, but I'm not a dummy either. I haven't gotten this far without knowing how to protect myself."

"What do you mean?" Priscilla asked. "How?"

"I keep a little pistol on the boat. Just in case, you know?

Priscilla narrowed her eyes. "I didn't think a felon could own a gun."

Calvin shrugged. "Depends on the state and stuff. If you can convince the FTA you're not a safety risk, they can let you get one legally. When I was running drugs, I saw some bad guys do some bad things, but I wasn't one of them. Even the bureau could see that."

It made sense. If he was afraid someone from his past still had a score to settle, he'd be crazy to travel around the world alone without any way to protect himself. Still, the idea of this man being armed didn't make Priscilla feel very comfortable.

"I don't like the idea of someone coming after you and putting Joan in danger," she said.

"I know." Calvin glanced at Joan. "I'll clear out after I deliver everything to Rayne Monday morning."

"But Calvin—"

"No, Joanie, it's for the best. I'll shake this guy and come back. If he follows me back here, then I'll get the police to step in. How'd that be?"

Joan didn't look very happy, but she nodded. "But will you be back by Christmas?"

"I'll do my very best. I've got a good setup with Rayne here on the island and, well..." He gave Joan another wink. "There are reasons I'd like to stick around."

Their eyes met for a moment, and then she turned to Priscilla.

"Is there anything else you'd like to ask before you go?"

It wasn't a very subtle hint.

Priscilla stood up. "I think that's all. Thanks for letting me stop by, Joan. And thank you, Calvin, for talking to me. I hope you'll be careful with my cousin."

"Don't you worry." Calvin stood too. "I'm just trying to keep my head down until I can deliver my cargo and get going."

Priscilla looked him up and down and then fixed her eyes on his. "Why don't you go now?"

"What?"

Joan frowned. "Priscilla."

"I mean it," Priscilla said. "Why not do it now? Or tomorrow sometime? Why wait till Monday?"

"Rayne isn't open till Monday," Joan said tightly.

"He could call her and have her let him in."

"I'm sorry," Calvin said, "but I can't do that. She told me she's got something to do tomorrow. I don't know what it is, but she's got something to do."

"She and her husband?" Priscilla asked.

"Yeah. Her husband. They're going onto the mainland for something. I don't know. A family thing. Christmas party or birthday, I don't know. Do you want me to call her and see for sure?"

"You can't bother her about that on a Saturday night," Joan protested.

"If it will be safer for Calvin than waiting around the island until Monday," Priscilla said. "I don't know why you wouldn't want him to."

Joan looked worriedly at Calvin.

"I'll call her. It's okay." He took out his phone and found Rayne's number on his list. "Hey, Rayne," he said when she picked up. "This is Calvin Gallico. Look, I'm over at Joan's right now. She and her cousin Priscilla are here, and we were talking about me maybe bringing the rest of my cargo over to your place tomorrow instead of Monday. It's fine by me, but I thought you had something tomorrow on the mainland. You and Donny."

Priscilla heard the low, indistinguishable murmur of Rayne's voice, and then Calvin nodded.

"Yeah, right. Right. I see. I wouldn't want to miss my aunt's birthday either, especially if it's a family reunion too. Well, you two have fun, and I'll see you first thing Monday. Have a good night." He ended the call and looked apologetically at Priscilla. "They're already heading to the mainland, and they'll be out all day tomorrow."

"Maybe you ought to leave anyway," Joan suggested. "Just to be safe. You can sell your things later on."

"Can't do it, Joanie. I have people coming. I wouldn't stay in business long if I did my customers like that. But don't worry. I don't think one extra day will make that big a difference. Justin hasn't found me yet."

"So Rayne's going to her aunt's birthday party?" Priscilla asked.

"Actually, it's her husband's aunt, but I can't ask her to miss something like that for me. Must be a pretty big affair for them if they're spending most of the weekend on it. Dinner tonight and then some family outing tomorrow."

"I guess so," Priscilla said, and under Joan's angry stare, she put on her coat and gloves. "Sorry to have kept you from your dinner. And both of you, please, be careful."

She hurried out to her SUV and got inside. That had been awkward. Maybe she'd been too hard on Calvin, too blunt, but the more she heard about him and his past, the more worried she became. Not only his past worried her, but his present and his future and how they were tied up with Joan's.

There had to be a way to check his story about Justin Weir, about his identity and about his intentions. Max Moran. That was the guy's name, Justin's supposed father. Justin had seemed harmless enough, but anyone could put up a good front. What could she do? He hadn't threatened Calvin. He hadn't said anything suspicious or done anything illegal—yet—but he did know Calvin by his old alias. Who was he exactly?

The police wouldn't have any reason to investigate him. Calvin's speculations about who he was and what he was after were just that, speculations. She needed someone who could make an unofficial inquiry. She needed Gerald.

CHAPTER FOURTEEN

Gerald probably wasn't going to be happy that Priscilla questioned Calvin about Justin Weir, but he ought to at least know what Calvin had said about him and that Calvin kept a gun aboard the *Barrett*. If Gerald was following his own line of inquiry, he didn't need to find out something like that at a dangerous moment. She'd have to call him.

She ran a couple of errands on the way home, took Jake for a quick, frigid walk, and then steeled herself to make her call to Gerald. But he called her first.

"Hey," she said when she answered the phone. "I was about to call you."

"I was hoping you'd be home. Everything okay?"

"Sure. Is there a reason it shouldn't be?"

"I know you weren't very happy with me last time we talked," he said. "I only wanted to make sure you weren't still mad."

"Not mad," she admitted, curling up on the couch in the heavy afghan that had been draped over one end. "Well, not really mad. I'm just concerned about everything that's happening and about what you're planning to do."

"What do you mean? I haven't got any plans."

Gerald wasn't the type to lie, but somehow she felt his denial was a little too emphatic.

"No plans at all?"

"Just keeping an eye on Calvin," he said. "Just to make sure there's nothing going on. That's about it."

"I thought maybe you were trying to figure out something to do to help Aggie out. Nothing?"

"Oh. That."

Yes, that. She knew *that* had to be on his mind all the time.

"Like I told you," he said when she merely waited for him to go on, "I'm working it out."

"Okay." She didn't have any right to demand more of an answer, as much as she would have liked to.

"Look," he said, his voice tightening, "I might have to do something I'd rather not, something I know might upset people if they knew about it, but I don't see any other way. Ava's got to have treatment, and I don't want Aggie and Nick going bankrupt over it. If I have to do something I don't want to do so I can help them, then that's okay."

She didn't like the sound of that, not one bit.

"I know they mean the world to you," she said, trying her best to keep calm. "But they wouldn't want you to do anything drastic on their account."

"I know. And I know you wouldn't either. That's why I'm keeping it to myself. Maybe I won't have to go through with it anyway. If not, why get everybody worried over it?"

This was sounding worse and worse. What kind of situation had he gotten himself into?

"I hope you're not planning on doing anything dangerous."

He laughed. "No, of course not. I know what I'm doing."

"Just be careful," she said. "Don't do anything crazy. Maybe I can help with Ava's expenses."

"No." His voice was suddenly hard. "I'm not going to let you do that. This is my family, and I'm the one to take care of them. Understand?"

"All right."

"Really," he said more gently. "I don't want you to worry. I know what I'm doing."

"All right," she said again, and there was an awkward silence. Jake nosed his way under the afghan with her and settled in her lap. She buried her fingers in his thick, warm fur.

"You said you were about to call me," he said at last. "What about?"

"I talked to Calvin just a little while ago."

"Priscilla."

"I know. You want me to stay out of it. This was something I had to ask him about."

"I don't want you going out to that boat by yourself. You don't need to be over there."

"I wasn't over there. Joan had him over for dinner tonight, and I went there to ask him about Justin Weir."

"What about him?"

"I just think it's weird that this guy looking for South American art would come looking for someone who fits Calvin's description and who uses the same name Calvin used to go by when he was smuggling drugs. It's too much of a coincidence if Calvin's not the man he's looking for."

"Okay, yeah, I agree. Does Calvin know him?"

"That's the part I wanted to tell you about. Calvin wasn't sure who he could be at first because he's too young to be someone he knew when he was dealing drugs, but after he thought about it for a while, he said he thinks Justin is the son of someone he worked with when he was in the drug business. A man named Max Moran. Did you read about him when you were researching Calvin?"

"No."

"Calvin said Moran was killed by the police during a raid that came about because of information Calvin gave them. He thinks Justin is after him because of that."

"I don't remember anything about that in the information I saw on Calvin's record. But I didn't read everything. Anyway, whatever happened was a long time ago. Is he sure about Justin?"

"Not entirely, but I can tell he's worried about him. But what can he do? He doesn't have much to go on. There's nothing the police would be interested in at this point."

"Didn't you already tell them about Justin's visit to Rayne's? I thought they were going to question him about that."

"They're supposed to," Priscilla said.

"Then you really should let them do their job. And let me do mine. I'll check into this Max Moran if I can, but there's probably nothing much I can find out at this point. Twenty years is a long time. I understand Calvin being a little bit paranoid after what he was involved with, but that's probably all it is."

"But Gerald—"

"Look, it's Christmastime, Rachel just moved closer to you, you've got your cousins right here on the island. Why not just relax and enjoy it all?"

Priscilla stroked Jake for a moment, glad he was there, warm and alive, with her. "I just wanted to let you know that Calvin keeps a gun on his boat."

It was a second or two before Gerald answered. "Okay. I'll keep that in mind. Thanks."

Thanks? That was all he had to say?

She exhaled slowly, not wanting her frustration to show in her voice. "Is Ava still doing all right?"

"Yeah. She's supposed to have surgery right after Christmas. The doctor wants to do it now, but Aggie doesn't want her to have to spend her first Christmas in the hospital. The doctor says a few days' wait won't hurt anything."

"I'm glad they're not going to do it until Christmas is over. They ought to enjoy the season." She bit her lip, glad he couldn't see the worry in her expression. "I want you to enjoy the season too."

"I will," he said. "As soon as I get all this worked out." His laugh wasn't all that convincing. "You take your own advice, okay?"

"I'll try."

None of this was very reassuring. Before she could think of anything else to say, her phone beeped.

"I'm sorry, but that's Rachel trying to get in touch with me. I guess I'd better take the call."

"Sure," Gerald said. "I'll talk to you soon."

He hung up before she could say anything else. She answered the still-beeping call. "Hello, darling."

"Hey, Mom. Listen, A.J. is taking me to hear the Boston Pops Christmas concert the day before Christmas Eve."

"Ooh, that sounds fun."

"It sounds wonderful," Rachel said, and Priscilla smiled a little, wondering how much of her daughter's dreamy sigh was due to the program and how much was due to her escort.

"So . . . where do things stand between you two? I know you're serious, but are we talking 'setting a date' serious?"

"Mom." Priscilla could practically hear Rachel roll her eyes. "It's just a concert."

"Uh-huh. And earlier it was just a visit to the Museum of Fine Arts and before that it was a tour of all the Revolutionary War sites and then—"

"All right! All right!" Rachel was laughing now. "I did move here to be with him. It's not like we don't go out all the time."

"And I bet you've spent some nights just having dinner and a movie or pizza at your place with a DVD."

"Yeah," she admitted, sounding almost shy now. "I guess."

"And, so?"

"Oh, Mom, I don't know. I like him so much. Okay, I love him so much. But it's a scary step to take. I mean, how do I know we're right for each other? There's so much more to being married than pizza and a DVD."

"I suppose you never know for sure. You think you know. You hope you know. But when it comes down to it, if you really want to stay together, you have to make up your mind that you'll work through whatever comes up together. As much as I loved your dad, there were always little things here and there, and big things sometimes too, that we had to figure our way through. And the only way we made it was to remember what we had promised each other the day we got married. It meant we didn't get our own way every time. Sometimes neither of us got what we wanted. But we did what was best for us together. If you can do that for A.J. and he can do that for you, then you'll do just fine."

"But how do I know he'll do that? How do I know he won't decide I'm not worth it? How do I know—"

"Rachel, darling, slow down. That's what this part of the relationship is for, when you're face-to-face on a day-to-day basis and not just behind a computer screen or on the phone. Before you make any promises, you see how he treats you when things don't go right. You see how he treats his family, especially his mother. You see how he honors his commitments to his friends and to his family and to his job. You see how he treats other people. Once the new wears off your relationship, that's how he'll treat you. And you are definitely worth being loved and cherished."

"Says everybody's mom."

Priscilla laughed. "No, not everybody's, but definitely yours. For now, though, don't worry. Just spend time with him and see how he is every day. If you don't see some flaws, then there's definitely something wrong."

"I'll keep that in mind. I've already noticed that he yells at the TV during hockey games."

"Well, that's probably not too serious," Priscilla said with a chuckle. "Just don't expect it to get any better if you two get married."

"It's okay. I yell too."

"Don't tell me you've started watching hockey!"

Rachel giggled. "I can't help it. I really enjoy it now."

"Goodness, it must be love. But I bet you didn't call me up to confess that you've learned to like hockey."

"Actually, I just wanted to talk to you about A. J. And tell you about the concert. Since it's the day before Christmas Eve, and I want to wear something especially nice. I wish you could come back to Boston and help me pick out something. And the shoes and jewelry and everything else to go with it."

"I wish I could, darling, but I really couldn't make the trip again so soon. I'm sure whatever you choose will be wonderful."

Priscilla hated to leave the island again while this thing with Calvin was going on. But then again, there didn't seem to be much she could do to figure it out either. Not until more information came to light. But maybe Gerald would say something tomorrow.

"Why don't you send me pictures of what you have in mind while you're shopping, and we can chat about it?"

"Okay. A.J. and I are going to his church," Rachel said, "but I'll call you tomorrow."

"That'll be perfect. We'll talk then."

After they said goodbye, Priscilla sat wrapped in her afghan for a few minutes longer. She had always believed the advice she'd just given her daughter. It proved valuable all those years ago when she and Gary first began to date. She'd thought it was still useful now that she and Gerald were getting to know each other, but maybe she was wrong. Maybe she didn't know him as well as she thought she did.

Gerald wasn't at church the next morning, which was unusual for him. None of the people he usually kept up with at church knew anything about where he might be, and Priscilla couldn't help wondering if his granddaughter's condition had taken a sudden turn for the worse.

The sermon was on how God provided for His people. Maybe He didn't give them exactly what they asked for, but He always gave them what they needed exactly when they needed it. It was precisely the message Priscilla needed to hear.

"Lord, keep us safe," she prayed as she began her drive home, "and help me know what to do next."

She felt restless somehow. She needed to go home and work on the quilt she was making for Joan for Christmas. She was cutting it close as it was, and it would be a near miracle if it was done on time, but somehow she couldn't stand the thought of sitting in the cottage all afternoon. She considered calling Rachel and seeing if she was already out looking for her new outfit, but she didn't feel like talking either. She ought to check on Gerald since he hadn't been at church, but she didn't feel like butting heads with him, especially over Calvin and Joan. She just needed some time to think, to shut down everything going on around her and just think.

She glanced at her watch. Jake was probably ready to go out, but it wouldn't be urgent yet. He was well trained. She passed by the turn toward home and headed instead to the road that ran along the ocean. There was something soothing about the regular ebb and flow of the tide, something hypnotic about the constant rush and crash of the waves that calmed her nerves and cleared her head. The sea was an icy gray shot with white—forbidding and yet somehow reassuring in its inexorable strength.

She pulled over somewhere near Makonikey and sat watching the water. It was impossible not to think of Calvin and his magnificent yacht. How exactly did he make his money? And what did Alessandra Alvarez and Justin Weir have to do with it? And why—

She blinked hard, not sure she was seeing what she thought she was seeing. That was Gerald walking on the beach. He wasn't in uniform, and there was another man with him, a man whose deep-mahogany skin made her think he was Latino. Of course there were a number of Latinos on the island, especially Brazilians, but somehow she didn't think this man was one of them. Maybe it was just because she had the situation with Calvin on her mind, but she couldn't help thinking this stranger resembled Alessandra Alvarez more than any of the Brazilians she had seen on Martha's Vineyard. Could he also be from Peru? Was it crazy to think he might be involved in whatever Calvin was bringing into the country?

She was sitting between two parked cars. It wasn't very likely that Gerald would notice her, but she could see him. He and the other man were talking. Gerald shrugged his shoulders. The other man reached into his pocket and brought out a roll of bills big enough to make Priscilla's mouth drop open. A van pulled in front of her, blocking her view for a minute. When it was gone, the money was nowhere to be seen and Gerald and the other man were shaking hands.

CHAPTER FIFTEEN

A minute later, the Latino man was standing on the dock watching Gerald climb into his SUV and head back toward Tisbury.

Priscilla bit her lip, not sure what to think. What was Gerald doing? Was this the "just a guy" he had spoken to on the telephone at his daughter's house a few days before? And what was the man paying him for?

"Oh, Lord," she breathed, "please don't let this be as bad as it looks."

Surely he wouldn't do anything illegal just because he needed money. Not Gerald. Please, Lord, not Gerald.

She thought hard about what she had seen. He'd been willing to help her find out what Calvin was doing. He'd even arranged to bring the dog to check out his yacht. But then he had spoken to Alessandra Alvarez. Unofficially, it seemed. Had he been getting information from her or warning her to leave Calvin alone? He had seemed eager for Priscilla to stop prying into Calvin's business after that. Had Calvin made a deal with him? Had he paid Gerald to look the other way when he brought in his contraband?

And who was this "just a guy" she had seen him with just now? Another South American it seemed. Was he really Peruvian? And what had he paid Gerald for? More looking the other way? Or was it to put him in contact with a known dealer here in Martha's Vineyard? If Gerald's business with this man was legitimate, then why had he come over here to talk to him rather than staying in Tisbury? Why hadn't he wanted to talk to him in front of Aggie?

The man drove away in a green late-model Chevy, and Priscilla turned the SUV toward home. She hardly knew it when she reached the cottage. Her hands were red from holding the steering wheel so tightly, and her head was throbbing. Instead of making this puzzle easier to solve, every new bit of information seemed to make it worse. Was everybody in on this drug ring?

Jake jumped up on her the minute she opened the door, and she petted his head absently. "All right, boy, we're going right now."

They set off down the street, and Priscilla's steps were even more brisk than usual. Brisk with the cold. Brisk with agitation.

It wasn't until she got back home that she realized Rachel had left a message for her on her cell phone. She had turned it off before church and had neglected to turn it on again. She couldn't help smiling at the sound of her daughter's carefree young voice.

"Hey, Mom. I guess you're busy, but I wanted to let you know that I found the cutest outfit at this little boutique just down the street from me. It's kind of…spangly and silvery, but not like a disco ball or anything. Great for Christmas and everything. I'll have to send you a picture when I get time. I found the perfect shoes for it too. Anyway, A.J. wants to go see a movie, so I'll call you later. Love you, Mom."

Still smiling, Priscilla hung up and then leaned down to set a match to the fire she had laid the night before. She ate a quick lunch and let the fire and a cup of hot coffee warm her up. That along with Rachel's message grounded her back into her everyday life where things made sense and people were who she thought they were. Okay, maybe she was misinterpreting everything she had just seen between Gerald and the Hispanic guy on the beach. Still, she couldn't see how. Why would that man give Gerald that kind of money?

She wanted to talk this out with someone. She needed to take the facts and lay them all out before someone who might be able to come up with a better explanation for them. An explanation that didn't involve a man she trusted and admired being involved with drug smugglers. But who could she talk to? Not Joan, obviously. She was too defensive about Calvin to think clearly. Not Rachel. Rachel didn't need anything to spoil this happy time of her life. There was Trudy, of course, and Gail, but Priscilla knew Trudy had some kind of luncheon with her church this afternoon. And Gail and her dad were supposed to visit some of her mother's relatives for an early Christmas party.

"Looks like it's you and me, Jake," Priscilla said, and he snuggled up beside her on the sofa as she got out her appliqué quilt and went to work. She'd have the whole afternoon to think.

Priscilla fell asleep on the couch at about nine thirty, her sewing still in her hands. She was hungry when she woke up an hour or so later, so she ate a quick bowl of soup, let Jake out, fed him, and then stumbled into bed. After a night of tossing and turning, she woke the next morning grouchy, still tired and still absolutely famished. Nothing in her refrigerator appealed to her, so she took Jake for a quick walk, gave him his breakfast, and then went into Tisbury.

She treated herself to a nice breakfast at Little House Café, then went over to Bea's Fabrics to get more of the blue thread she was running low on. She was surprised to see Mildred there looking at a collection of colonial reproduction fabrics.

"Mildred." Priscilla went over to her. "I almost didn't recognize you in civilian clothes."

Mildred smiled down at her practical slacks and down jacket. "I have to admit, I always feel a little out of place in anything more recent than 1860. How are you?"

"Oh, fine. Trying to finish up an appliqué quilt for a Christmas present, and I seem to be running out of time."

"Goodness. How far along are you?"

Priscilla sighed. "I've finished all the blocks and borders, and now I'm working on the actual quilting."

Mildred winced. "Maybe you'd better just give it as is and promise to make it into a quilt sometime after Christmas."

"I may have to do that, but I'm going to try to get it done in time. Best I can anyway. There always seems to be something going on that I have to take care of first."

"I know how that is."

Priscilla looked around the shop, then moved closer to her friend. "I didn't expect to see you here, but since you are, I was wondering if I could ask you something."

"Sure. Fire away."

"Remember the guy who came into your museum asking about South American art?"

"The one with the ponytail?" Mildred asked. "Sure. Why?"

"I was wondering if you'd heard from him again."

Mildred shook her head. "I thought you sent him over to Rayne's."

"Yeah, he's been there. I just wondered if you'd seen him again."

"Did he buy anything from her?" Mildred asked. "I hope so. Poor thing, she could use the business."

Priscilla frowned. "What do you mean?"

Mildred hesitated for a minute. "I don't like to talk about anybody's personal problems, but I just feel bad for her. I'd like to do something for her, or maybe get a few people to pitch in together. Just until she can get on her feet again. It's hard enough trying to run a business on your own without having to deal with divorce too."

"What do you mean? Is Rayne getting divorced?"

"Didn't you know? Her husband took off three or four months ago and moved in with some girl half his age. He emptied their bank account, sold off everything he could, and just took off. Don't mention this to anyone. I'm sure she doesn't want it getting around, but I feel awful for her. I don't know how she makes it in that tiny little gallery without any help."

Priscilla could hardly believe what she was hearing. Rayne never went more than a few minutes without mentioning her amazing paragon of a husband. He was always worried about her, fussing over her, providing for her, encouraging her to follow her dreams.

"How do you know this?" Priscilla asked, a tremor in her voice. "Are you sure Rayne's the one you heard about? I don't like to gossip about people, but this is important. I need to know for sure if this is true."

"A friend of mine lives on her street, and her husband and Rayne's played golf. Evidently, Rayne's husband told my friend's husband all about it when he decided to leave. He'd planned it all out and just took off. Never looked back."

This was bad. This was very bad.

"You're sure it was Rayne's husband, Donovan Forster."

Mildred looked a little uncertain. "Well, I didn't see for myself, if that's what you mean, but that's what my friend said. She told me she tried to talk to Rayne, to see if she could do anything to help, but Rayne didn't want to talk about it. As I said, that was three or four months ago. Donovan hasn't been back to the house as far as anyone there has seen."

Very, very bad.

Priscilla glanced at her watch. Calvin ought to have delivered those crates to Rayne's by now. Whatever was going on here had to have something to do with them, something to do with Rayne. She had clearly been lying to Priscilla all this time, but lying about how much?

"Listen, Mildred, I've got to go. Thanks for telling me about Rayne. I promise I didn't ask just to hear a juicy story. This might be really important."

"Important?" Mildred looked alarmed now. "What do you mean? What's wrong?"

"I'll have to catch you up later."

Priscilla checked her watch again, then hurried out of the shop and back to the SUV. The minute she was inside, she turned on the engine to get the heater running, then got out her phone.

"Trudy," she said breathlessly when her cousin answered the phone. "Are you home?"

"Sure! What's wrong? Where are you?"

"I'm at the fabric shop, Bea's. Can I come over?"

"Sure, come on over!" Trudy's voice was more emphatic than usual. "Is everything all right?"

"Give me a minute. I'll be right there."

The instant Priscilla pulled up in front of Trudy's house, the door flew open and Trudy rushed outside.

"What is it? What's wrong?"

"Let's go in." Priscilla hurried her back up to the house and inside. "Are you busy right now? Do you have a few minutes to help me with something?"

Trudy's blue eyes sparkled. "Is it about your investigation? Are we going under cover?"

"Calm down. It's not that big a deal. I just found out that Rayne hasn't been telling me the truth about some things and I—"

"Ooh, what?"

"I don't want to say anything about that unless I have to."

Trudy's face fell. "You're no fun."

"This is serious. I mean it. It doesn't matter what she's been lying about, just that she's been lying. I'd really like to get a good look at whatever it is Calvin left at her studio this morning, and I need you to help me do that."

"The drugs?" Trudy's eyebrows went up. "You don't think it's dangerous, do you?"

"I don't think it's drugs," Priscilla said. "We didn't find any sign of them on Calvin's yacht, but there's definitely something, and I want to know what it is."

"What do you want me to do?"

Priscilla looked her in the eye. "Do you think you could distract Rayne for a few minutes?"

"Distract her?"

"Just talk to her. About her art or something. Just keep her focused on some of the things she's made. Ask her what she thought about when she was making them or which artists most influenced her work or whatever. Or tell her about Joan's paintings and ask her if she thinks Joan might have a future as an artist. Do you think you could do that?"

Trudy nodded, for once saying nothing.

"Are you free to go now?"

Again Trudy nodded.

"Let's go then."

Trudy bundled up, and they headed out toward Rayne's gallery.

"Do you think we ought to tell somebody where we're going?" Trudy asked when they were about halfway there. "Gerald maybe?"

Not Gerald. It couldn't be Gerald. As much as Priscilla wanted to rely on him, she just couldn't. Not after what she had seen yesterday. If Gerald was on the take— No, she wouldn't think that. She'd find out what was happening on her own. It was just Rayne after all.

CHAPTER SIXTEEN

Priscilla made sure to park at the front of the gallery, right where everyone could see. If something happened, at least someone would know she had been there.

"Are you sure we should do this?" There was a little shiver in Trudy's voice.

Priscilla stopped with her hand on the frosted metal of the gallery door handle. "Would you rather not? Believe me, I completely understand if you want to get back in the car. I don't want you to do anything you don't feel comfortable about."

"Comfortable?" Trudy's lips twitched a little. "I don't guess something like this is ever likely to feel comfortable, but I'm all right. If you think it's okay, then I'm with you!"

"Great. And remember, you don't have to do anything but talk. Just keep her attention on the pieces in the gallery, and I'll do the rest."

"Got it." Trudy lifted her chin and put back her shoulders. "Let's go."

The bell over the door gave a brittle, frigid jingle as they stepped inside.

"Rayne?" Priscilla called when she saw no one. "Are you here?"

There was absolute silence in the place. For a moment, Priscilla imagined Rayne lying dead in her studio, victim of ruthless drug smugglers, but an instant later Rayne came into the gallery, her smock and hands covered with grime but a smile on her always-expressive face.

"Priscilla. I thought that might be you. And Trudy. How are you both?"

"Hi there," Priscilla said. "I hope you don't mind us dropping in, but we were talking about some of the things you have on display here and thought we'd come by to see them again. They're so unusual and thought provoking, we never can agree on what some of them really mean."

Priscilla strolled over to the sculpture of the woman's head with the ruined Paris street inside. The meaning was crystal clear now, romance, beauty, dreams, love, all abandoned, all left to fall into ruin. Whatever else Rayne had done or was doing now, Priscilla couldn't help feeling sorry for her. How betrayed and humiliated she must have felt when her husband took off.

Priscilla kept a smile on her face, reminding herself that she didn't know any actual details about Rayne's husband or their marriage. She didn't really know how Rayne had felt. Was feeling. Right now she had a job to do.

"I know you said you don't like to explain your pieces," she said, still admiring the skill and the emotion that had gone into the creation of the sculpture. "But this one fascinates me. Was there something in particular that inspired it?"

Rayne gave them a Mona Lisa smile. "Life. There is no art without the joy and pain and terror of life. But there are many aspects to it. People almost always tell me this piece makes them feel sad. But then there's this one..." She led them over to a painting that hadn't been in the gallery the last time Priscilla had been there. "This one is all light and joy and hope."

The painting was of a mother and child running on a beach, sunlit and laughing, the water almost as golden as the sand. Priscilla tried not to let her thoughts show in her face, but now she wondered. Surely not.

"It's lovely," she said. "Do you like it, Trudy?"

"It's beautiful!" Trudy looked up at it, genuine admiration in her eyes. "It makes me feel warmer just to look at it. How do you do that? How do you make it seem so alive?"

There was something sadly grateful in Rayne's expression. How badly she must need to feel someone's affirmation after what she had gone through and with what lay ahead. "It makes me very happy to hear you say that."

"My sister, Joan, is a painter," Trudy said. "I know it always makes her happy when someone appreciates her work."

"As an artist—"

"I'm so sorry to interrupt," Priscilla said, "but is there a restroom I could use?"

"Oh, sure." Rayne nodded toward the half-open door at the back of the gallery. "In the studio, the little door in the back right corner."

"Thanks. Be right back."

Priscilla crept away as quickly as possible, leaving Trudy and Rayne still looking at the painting, their backs to the studio door.

"What were you saying about being an artist?" Trudy asked.

"Well, just that, as an artist, it means a lot to me to know that people like my work and that they feel something when they look at it. I spend a lot of time on each one of my pieces, not just creating it but planning it. It can be very lonely work, but it makes it all worthwhile when someone understands what it means, when someone..."

The words became indistinguishable as Priscilla passed through the doorway into the studio. There was the stack of crates that had been in Calvin's yacht the week before. She didn't dare stop to look at them yet, even though two of them had had their lids removed and she could see the straw that protected the fragile contents and even a tantalizing bit of earthenware among it. First things first.

She hurried to the door in the back right corner, opened it and then closed it firmly. She was careful not to slam it. No use being too obvious. That done, she crept back to the opposite side of the studio, making sure as she passed the door that Trudy was still talking to Rayne. Trudy was her usual animated self, gesturing toward the painting of the mother and child, and judging by the lilt in her voice, asking more questions. Good.

Priscilla edged over to the stack of crates. Rayne would have to come all the way into the studio to see her now, but she couldn't take too long here and give herself away. As carefully and silently as she could manage, Priscilla pushed the straw away from one of the clay jugs and lifted it out of the crate. It was perhaps two feet tall, half as wide, with a neck that tapered down to a mere two or three inches. It was impossible to see anything but darkness inside.

Unsure what to do now, she held the jug in both hands and gave it a sharp jolt. She was sure something shifted inside. There wasn't a rattle as if there was something loose in there. It was more of a rustle. What could it be? She glanced toward the door again. Trudy was still talking, but Priscilla would have to go back in a minute or two. Rayne would start to wonder where she was.

But she had to try to see what was in that jug. She laid it back on the straw and rummaged in her purse. There was a little flashlight on a chain she kept for emergencies. That ought to do nicely. She looped the chain around her finger and then picked up the jug again. What was in there? What could Calvin possibly be—

"Priscilla!"

Priscilla flinched at Rayne's horrified cry, and the jug slipped through her hands. She clutched at it and then clutched at empty air as it shattered on the studio's cement floor. Out of it rolled something packed in straw, straw that immediately fell away, and Priscilla caught a startled breath.

"Don't!" Rayne cried, rushing toward it, and behind her Trudy shrieked.

It was a human skull.

CHAPTER SEVENTEEN

What are you doing?" Priscilla gasped, still staring at the skull. "What have you done? Who is that?"

"Priscilla," Trudy breathed, her face dead white.

"Get out, Trudy! Go! Get the police!"

"No!" Rayne wrung her hands helplessly. "Please, wait. It's not what it looks like. Please, just let me explain."

"Priscilla," Trudy repeated.

Priscilla looked at her and then back at Rayne. "Whatever this is, the police are going to have to know about it."

Tears sprang to Rayne's dark eyes. "Please don't tell anyone. Please. I'll stop. I promise I will."

Trudy managed to look more horrified than she had already. "Wh-what have you been doing?"

"Trudy," Priscilla ordered, "go to the front door."

"Please!" Rayne held up her clasped hands. "Please let me just explain all this. Please."

"Go to the front door, Trudy," Priscilla repeated, and then she turned to Rayne again. "We'll listen, but we're not going to stand back here out of sight while we do it, agreed?"

Rayne nodded miserably. The skull lay against one of Calvin's crates, giving them a malicious, eyeless grin.

"And you'd better leave things back here just the way they are for now."

Priscilla was more than happy to follow Rayne and Trudy back into the relative normalcy of the gallery.

"You stand right by the door, Trudy," Priscilla said. "If you feel the least bit uncomfortable, go out and get help."

"I already feel uncomfortable," Trudy said, hugging herself.

"No, really," Rayne said, wiping her eyes on the hem of her smock. "You don't have to be afraid. I'd never hurt anyone, I swear. That's—that's not what you think it is."

Priscilla pressed her mouth into a grim line, mostly to keep her lips from trembling. "Are you saying that skull is fake?"

Rayne sniffled and shook her head. "No, it's real. It's human."

"Whose is it? What happened?"

"I don't know whose it is. I just—"

"How can you not know whose skull you just happen to have?" Trudy squeaked.

"It's not like that," Rayne said. "Whoever that is, he died centuries ago."

Priscilla's eyebrows went up. "Centuries?"

Rayne nodded. "There are people who are willing to pay a lot of money for ancient artifacts. The governments of the places these artifacts come from don't very much like it when they're taken away and sold to people in other places. Some of them come from ancient burial grounds, many of them are sacred to the people who buried them, all of them are important to the history of the places they come from. Usually, the only way collectors can get ahold of them is to have them smuggled into the country. That's what Calvin does. He finds natives of the countries he goes to and pays them to bring him artifacts. Then he brings them back to the US and sells them."

"Where do you fit in?" Priscilla asked.

"I didn't even know about any of this until this morning. I had no idea what he was doing. He was bringing the crates in like he always does, but he dropped one and it busted open. When I saw what was inside the piece that shattered, I knew something was going on—it wasn't a skull, but I knew that he was smuggling something in. Calvin told me if I didn't tell anyone he'd make it worth my while, and that maybe we could even do this as a regular thing." Rayne bit her lip and looked upward, her eyes still brimming with tears. "This is the first time I've ever done this, honest. I...I guess I didn't know what to do. I have some personal problems, and I don't know how I'm going to keep the gallery going. I'd just about decided I was going to have to sell everything and close up." She pushed her wild curls away from her face. "If he'd made the offer last month or even last week, I would never have given it a second thought. But right then..."

She held out beseeching hands.

"I understand your husband left you," Priscilla said as gently as she was able. "I know that must have been upsetting for you."

"I don't know how you know that, but, yes, he left." She looked pleadingly at Priscilla. "He just left."

"I'm so sorry," Trudy murmured.

"But that wasn't all. That was bad, I know, but I can take care of myself. I always have. If I had to sell this place and the house and start over in a little studio somewhere, I could manage. I've done it before, but now…"

Again she trailed off, her voice choked to nothing.

"But now you're going to have a baby," Priscilla said softly.

Trudy caught her breath.

The tears in Rayne's eyes spilled over. "How did you know?"

"I wasn't really sure," Priscilla admitted, "but I saw your face when you were talking about that sculpture of the woman's head when I already knew about your husband leaving, and then I saw how it changed when you described your new painting of the mother and child on the beach."

"I'm not young anymore," Rayne said pensively, "but I've always hoped for a baby. Donovan didn't want children, so I guess it's a little ironic that I should be expecting now, but I don't care. I'm glad. I just didn't know what to do to pay for everything on my own. I thought this deal with Calvin was the answer. I mean, it's not like we're really hurting anyone. It's not like selling drugs."

"It's still against the law," Priscilla said. "And there are people in the countries these things were taken from who are very upset about having them sold off."

Trudy glanced uncertainly toward the door into the studio. "What else is in there?"

"I don't even know," Rayne said, drying her eyes again on her smock and pulling herself together. "I think the piece I saw this morning must have been some kind of idol once upon a time. Calvin told me there's an entire skeleton inside the crates in the studio now and some ceremonial robes. I don't know." She sighed heavily and then dropped into a chair that had been placed near the door. "What am I going to do now?"

"I don't know." Priscilla gave her a sympathetic pat on the back. "I'm sure the authorities will have something to say about that, though I'd guess that if you were to cooperate with them and help them put Calvin out of business, they'd go easier on you. Especially in your condition."

Rayne put a caressing hand over her stomach. "I'd hate to think of someone else raising my baby while I'm in prison."

"Maybe it won't come to that," Priscilla said. "Obviously, you didn't make a really smart choice when you decided to help Calvin with his operation, but I'd bet most people would understand why you did it. And maybe some of the things can be recovered and returned to their rightful places."

"That's the problem. I don't know anything about the buyers. I recorded the transactions and took their money, but it was all cash. And it was before I knew what they were really buying."

"All you can do is tell them what you know," Priscilla assured her. "They'll take care of the rest. They'll make sure Calvin—"

Trudy tugged her sleeve and then pointed out the front window. "It's him. And Joan is with him. What do we do?"

The two of them were headed straight for Rayne's door, laughing and talking as they came from Joan's car. Calvin was carrying a small wooden box.

"Don't say anything," Priscilla said, determined to keep a cool head. "Act like everything is the same as before. Just make small talk, and we'll hustle Joan out of here and go to the police. Are you going to be okay with him, Rayne?"

She nodded. "I'll tell him I broke the jug when I heard you at the door and that I've been talking to you out here ever since so you wouldn't come into the studio." She gave them a grim smile. "I've gotten pretty good at lying with a straight face lately."

"Okay, here they are."

There was a jingle of the bell and a blast of cold air as the door swung open and Calvin and Joan came in.

Joan hurried over to hug Trudy and Priscilla. "I didn't expect to find you here. Calvin and I were about to have lunch at the Lobster Shack, but he remembered part of his cargo he didn't bring over here this morning, so we thought we'd just drop it off."

"Don't want any of my customers to be disappointed," Calvin said, patting the little box. "I'll just put it with the other things in the back."

"Oh no you don't," Joan said, taking the box from him. "You'll spend half an hour checking all the stuff and making sure it's packed right. I'll do it."

Trudy's eyes widened as Joan strode toward the studio door. "Uh, Joan?"

"Don't you want to see Rayne's new painting first?" Priscilla asked, but it was too late. A muffled scream from the other room made it obvious that Joan had already seen the broken pottery and the skull.

Calvin bolted into the studio and pulled Joan back into the gallery with him.

"What's that doing there?" she asked, trying to pull away from him. "Who is it? What's going on?"

"That's what I'd like to know," Calvin barked. "What's been going on here, Rayne?" He glared at Priscilla. "No, don't even tell me. It was you, wasn't it? Miss Busybody just had to go poking around in other people's business."

Priscilla lifted her chin, glaring right back at him. "We know everything, and we're going straight to the police about it. Joan, come over here."

"Oh-ho no." Calvin kept his grip on Joan's arm and reached into his overcoat pocket with his free hand. "I had the foresight to bring my health insurance with me on this visit."

Joan gasped. "You brought your gun?"

"I never leave it behind when I'm making a delivery. Looks like I'm actually going to need it today."

Joan tried again to free herself, but she couldn't. "Calvin, you're hurting me. Calvin!"

"Be still and you won't be hurt."

Joan looked stunned. "What are you going to do? You wouldn't hurt anybody, would you?"

"Not if they don't get in my way, but I don't think they will. Not as long as I have you with me."

"Calvin," Joan breathed. "You—you can't. I thought you were a Christian. I thought you cared about me. I thought you and I—"

"Yeah, honey, that's what you get for thinking. Now open that door."

"Let her go!" Trudy said fiercely. "Run away if you want to, but let her go first."

"Out of the way." Calvin gestured toward the door with the hand in his pocket, and the outline of the pistol was distinct. "Go on and open it, Joan."

Priscilla put one hand on Trudy's shoulder. "Don't make it worse. We don't want to put Joan in more danger."

"Smart girl," Calvin said, his grin returning. "You just stay nice and quiet, and when I get somewhere safe, I'll send Cousin Joan back to you." He pulled Joan a little closer to the door and then turned back one last time to Rayne. "I was afraid I couldn't count on you. No wonder that husband of yours ditched you."

"Don't do this," Rayne pleaded. "Just let her go. We won't say anything to the police until you've had time to get away. We promise."

Priscilla still glared at him, saying nothing.

"Joan," Trudy said, reaching toward her sister.

Joan could only look back at her, fear in her eyes.

"Just stay where you are, all of you," Calvin said. "Say what you want to whoever you want. Just know it's up to you whether anything happens to little Joanie here, understand?"

No one replied to that. What could they say? Anything they did was likely to get someone hurt or killed. They merely watched as Calvin walked arm in arm with Joan back to her sedan as if they were taking a sweethearts' stroll. He walked her around to the driver's side door and nodded for her to get in and navigate over the center console before, sliding behind the wheel after her. With one hand, he started the car. His other hand was no doubt still in his overcoat pocket with his "health insurance."

Oh, Lord, Priscilla prayed as he drove away, a silent cry. *Help us.*

"What do we do?" Trudy asked. "What do we do?"

Priscilla dragged her keys out of her purse. "I'm going after them."

"You can't! You know what he said!"

"I'm not going to do anything. I just want to see where he goes."

"Priscilla—"

"I don't have time to talk. You call the police and tell them what happened. Tell them he has a gun and that he has a hostage. I'm pretty sure he'll be heading toward his yacht, but I don't want to lose sight of them." Priscilla pulled open the door, feeling the slap of the wet and cold. "The *Barrett*. Remember to tell them that."

Over Trudy's and Rayne's protests, Priscilla hurried out to her SUV and waited until she saw Joan's car turn out of sight. Calvin was headed to where the *Barrett* was docked, she was sure of that. She wasn't going to let him go anywhere else. Not with Joan.

She drove to where Calvin had turned and spotted Joan's sedan farther down the road. Eventually he turned on the road that went down to the Grahams' house and then around to the dock. Priscilla slowed to a stop on the far side of the house, hoping he wouldn't notice her, and waited to see him get out of the car and go around to the passenger side. Still with one hand in his overcoat pocket, he opened the door and gestured for Joan to get out.

She did what he wanted and then stopped there beside the car, chin lifted, mouth in a determined line, defiance in every line of her small frame, but Calvin merely grabbed her arm and pulled her toward the dock. They were about halfway there when, to Priscilla's amazement, Gerald's SUV pulled out from beside the Grahams' garage and stopped next to Joan's sedan. Gerald got out and said something to Calvin, Calvin nodded toward the yacht, and Gerald stepped aside to let them pass.

"No," Priscilla whispered, pounding her steering wheel with both hands.

He was helping Calvin. Gerald was helping him. It didn't matter that she understood why, that she understood how much it meant to him to help out his family. He was letting a criminal kidnap Joan. She tried to convince herself that it wasn't what it looked like, that he and Calvin had merely exchanged a word or two and that Calvin had convinced him that he and Joan were just going aboard to relax for a while.

No. It wouldn't do. Just the expression on Joan's face was enough to let anyone with a brain and half a heart know something was wrong.

Priscilla waited until the *Barrett* pulled away from the dock and headed out into open waters before she leaped out of her car and stalked over to where Gerald stood watching, a grim hardness in every line of his face.

"What are you doing?" she demanded, her face hot even with the cold wind from the sea buffeting her. "Are you out of your mind? Aggie would never want this kind of money no matter what the situation is. If I hadn't seen this with my own eyes, if I hadn't seen you let that—that monster kidnap Joan right in front of your eyes, I wouldn't have believed it." Her fists were clenched so tight, she could feel her nails cutting into the palms of her hands." Sudden tears fell warm onto her cheeks. "I trusted you, Gerald. I thought you were the kind of man—"

"What are you talking about?" His voice was harsh enough to make her jump. "I didn't *let* anyone do anything. He has a gun. I thought maybe I could make him see reason, but I wasn't going to risk my life or Joan's trying to take a weapon from him. Just what is it you think I've done?"

She blinked up at him, confused now. "You didn't take money to let him smuggle things into the country without being bothered by the Coast Guard?"

"I didn't what?" Gerald gaped at her. "How in the world did you get that idea?"

"Well, you wanted me to stop investigating him."

"For your own safety. I told you that."

"And you were talking to Alessandra Alvarez."

Gerald frowned. "What's that got to do with it?"

"She's Guadalupe's sister, the girl who got killed because of the evidence Calvin gave the police."

"I told you I didn't see any reference to a Guadalupe in Calvin's file. Why would I talk to Alessandra?"

Priscilla pursed her lips. "Why don't you tell me? I saw you with her."

He ran one hand through the crisp curls at the back of his neck. "That's not something I can talk about right now."

"I see," she said tautly. "You've told me you'd do anything to help Aggie out. And you said you were working on a plan to help her. Was Alessandra the plan? Or was it the man you took money from on the beach at Makonikey?"

He looked at her warily. "I don't know what you think you saw, but we'll have to worry about that later. Right now we've got to make sure Joan is okay."

"But she and Calvin'll be out of sight in a few more minutes."

"Trudy called me and told me what was going on. I wanted to try to stop Calvin before he got Joan on the yacht, but I called the station too. The patrol will be after them any time now."

Priscilla bit her lip, watching as the *Barrett* grew smaller and smaller in the distance, not knowing what to think about Gerald and what he had been up to. She couldn't worry about him just now. Joan was getting farther away, and there was no sign of a Coast Guard cutter anywhere.

"Gerald," she began, and then words failed her.

Without any reason she could see, the *Barrett* began to turn. It made a wide arc in the slate-colored waves and turned again toward the island. She looked at Gerald, but judging from his furrowed brow and frown, he was as puzzled as she was.

"What's he doing?" she asked, her voice low though Calvin couldn't possible hear her. "Why's he turning back?"

"I don't know." Gerald took a few steps toward the end of the dock, squinting into the faint sun. "It doesn't sound like engine trouble."

Priscilla could hear the faraway sound of the yacht's engines, clearly in working order. "You don't think somehow Joan—"

"Joan overpowered him or something?" Gerald laughed humorlessly. "Not very likely. We'll just have to wait and see."

There was a sudden dread in the pit of Priscilla's stomach. "He couldn't have shot her."

"He wouldn't come back here if he had," Gerald said, and then he nodded to their left. "Whatever's going on, we have backup now."

Two Coast Guard cutters were approaching the *Barrett*. Calvin wouldn't be making his escape by sea at any rate. Before they could draw near, the yacht pulled up to the dock again. The engine stopped. A few seconds later, Calvin came out onto the deck, his gloved hands raised over his head. Behind him was Joan, her arms crossed over her chest in disgust, her dark eyes full of contempt as they rested on him, but she didn't have a gun. *The* gun. Clearly, Calvin didn't either. Then why—

Emerging from the cabin was their answer. Behind them, a pistol trained on Calvin's back, was Alessandra Alvarez. She waved the gun at him, and he secured the yacht. All three of them filed off the boat onto the dock.

"Joan!" Priscilla cried.

Her cousin ran straight to her, clutching her hands. Priscilla could feel her trembling.

"Are you all right?"

Joan nodded, still glaring at Calvin.

"You'd better let me see to him now." Gerald took the gun from Alessandra. "Until they can take him into custody."

Seeing that the cutters had docked and some of the Guardsmen were heading toward them, she smiled grimly. "At least now I can find out what I need to know."

"What do you mean?" Priscilla asked. "What do you need to know? I thought your sister—"

"My sister?" Alessandra asked, puzzled. "I have no sister."

"But Guadalupe—"

Alessandra began to laugh now. "Guadalupe is a town in Peru. It is where Gallico meets with the people who rob our country of its history and its culture and sell it merely to please acquisitive foreign collectors and to line his filthy pockets."

"I didn't steal from any of those guys," Calvin said. "I paid for everything I got, and that's the truth."

"And you didn't care whether that was illegal in your country and mine or if anyone you bought it from had stolen it in the first place," Alessandra said, her dark face the picture of contempt. "You didn't care whose graves were ransacked or whose temples." Her black eyes flashed. "Or whose homeland."

Calvin merely huffed.

Alessandra turned again to Priscilla. "We finally tracked down the people from my own country who were selling our history and culture. My job now is to see how many of those artifacts I can recover and bring back home." She looked disdainfully at Calvin.

"And make sure the one responsible for bringing them to your country won't be able to do any more smuggling."

Priscilla's eyebrows went up. "You work for the Peruvian government."

Alessandra nodded. "I've been waiting for a good opportunity to search the *Barrett*. When I saw Gallico had taken the wrap off the boat, I knew he must be about to leave the island. I thought I'd better see what was aboard while I still had a chance. Even though I didn't find what I was looking for, it turned out quite well."

"And everything he told us about Guadalupe being your sister was a lie," Joan said, the color coming back into her pale face.

"I fear so," Alessandra said.

Joan turned on Calvin. "I believed you. You made me feel sorry for you. You made me defend you to people who were trying to tell me what a con man you are, people who actually care about me." Her voice shook. "You convinced me you were a Christian."

"Oh, get over yourself," Calvin snapped. "It wouldn't have worked if you hadn't wanted to believe it so bad."

Joan's lips trembled. Priscilla didn't know if she was going to cry or scream at him. Or maybe she was going to slap him. Instead she turned to Priscilla.

"I'd like to go home now."

"Of course," Priscilla said with all the warmth and understanding she could convey. She turned back to Gerald. "I can see you've got this. Maybe we can talk later?"

He looked at her, stone-faced. "Okay. I know I have some questions I need answers to."

He gave Joan a hug. "Thank God you're back safe and sound, Joan. The police will want to keep your car for a few hours since it's part of a crime scene. Priscilla can take you home, and we'll bring your car to you later."

Priscilla took Joan's arm. "I think," she said to Alessandra, "that you'll find the answers you want, at least some of them, at Rayne Forster's gallery."

"I will be going there right away." Alessandra's eyes were warm. "And I have a feeling you've had more to do with clearing this matter up than I know yet. Thank you."

Priscilla looked at Gerald again. "I don't know about that, but I'm glad to have helped stop people like him from doing any more damage to innocent people. Come on, Joan."

She hurried Joan to the car. Joan didn't look at her as they drove away. She didn't say anything. She merely stared straight ahead, not looking back to where Calvin was being handcuffed by the Guardsmen.

When they pulled up in front of Joan's cottage, Priscilla turned off the engine and went up to the door with her.

"Do you want me to come in for a while?" she asked. "I need to call Trudy and Gail. They'll be worried."

Joan nodded as she unlocked the door. Sister gave a happy little yip from her crate, and Joan immediately let her out, kneeling to hug her as she wriggled her whole body and licked Joan's face.

"I know," Joan murmured into her thick fur. "I'm glad I'm home too."

Priscilla hovered near the door, not sure whether Joan wanted her to stay or go. Joan finally looked up.

"Do me a favor and talk to Gail for me, will you? I'll call Trudy."

Between the four of them, in two overlapping conversations, they decided Trudy and Gail would come over to Joan's, both of them bringing a few things for a potluck dinner, to give them all an opportunity to talk about what had happened with Calvin and Alessandra.

"Don't come until after the police are through with me," Joan told Trudy. "I know you want to come over now, but you might as well wait. I'm fine. Priscilla's here with me. Everything is okay. You don't need to worry."

Priscilla had already finished her conversation with Gail, and she could hear Trudy's excited tones from Joan's phone.

Joan sighed. "Yes, I suppose they will. All right. I have to take Sister out, so I'll call you when I get back. I know." She smiled faintly. "Yes. And thank you."

Priscilla looked at her inquiringly once she had ended the call.

"She wants to come over now," Joan said. "She wants to tell us about what happened after you left Rayne's."

"I definitely want to know about that."

Joan nodded. "First I have to take Sister for a walk. Want to come?"

"I'd like that a lot."

CHAPTER EIGHTEEN

Priscilla and Joan were still bundled in their coats, gloves, and hats, so only a moment later they were walking swiftly down the sidewalk in front of Joan's cottage with Sister capering alongside. They had almost reached the cottage again before Joan finally said something.

"I guess I deserve a huge 'I told you so' from you and everybody."

"Of course not." Priscilla gave her gloved hand a comforting squeeze. "It's not your fault he's such a good liar. And it's not wrong for you to want to believe the best about someone and that people can turn their lives around. Where would any of us be if we didn't believe that?"

"But I feel so stupid." Joan sniffled and blinked hard in the whipping wind. "I'm not usually so easy to fool. I don't usually…"

She let the words trail off unfinished, but Priscilla could read them in her eyes. *I don't usually think someone could really be interested in me. I don't usually allow myself to think anything but practical thoughts. I don't usually let myself dream.*

"I'm so sorry," Priscilla said, hardly knowing what else to say. "But just because this guy was a jerk doesn't mean there's not someone out there who would truly love and appreciate you."

Joan made a little scoffing sound. "Easy for you to talk about 'someone out there' for me, but you don't believe there's someone for you even though Gerald is standing right there waiting for you to let him know you're interested."

Priscilla looked down at her feet as they swiftly covered the icy walkway. "I don't know about that."

"Oh, yes you do."

"I thought so a time or two," Priscilla admitted, her tone a bit more wistful than she would have liked it to be. "But I don't know now. Not after what I accused him of."

"Don't be silly. I don't know what you accused him of, but you two will work it out."

They turned up the walk to the cottage and hurried inside. Sister immediately plopped herself down on the couch, and Joan called Trudy to let her know they were back. Then she got a fire going in the fireplace.

"I was going to do this for Calvin and me after we had lunch," she said, watching the spark of red burst into crackling flame, and a tear slipped down her cheek, disappearing into her festive sweater before she could dash it away. "I feel so stupid. Stupid and ugly and old."

"Oh, Joan." Priscilla sank down onto the floor beside her and wrapped her arms around her cousin. "It's not true. It's not. You can't let someone like him steal your peace of mind like that. He's the one who ought to feel bad, not you. You're a wonderful person. You're not stupid and you're not ugly, and you're only old if you let yourself think so. Neither of us is a spring chicken anymore, but that doesn't mean our lives are over. That doesn't mean it's too late for us to find love if we want to. You were perfectly happy just as you were before you met Calvin. Why should you let someone like that, someone who preys on other people, make you feel like you're less than you were then?"

"I didn't want to believe him at first." Joan grabbed a tissue from the box on the end table and blotted her eyes with it. "I thought he was just teasing me about running away together, just kidding around, you know? And then I thought he just wanted a friend, someone who'd believe in him, someone who'd see how much he'd changed. And then—" She shook her head, the tears coming again. "He never said anything specific about being interested in me. He'd just say little things once in a while that made me think that's what he had on his mind. I didn't dare act like I thought it was anything but fun. I can't say that I loved him. But I was flattered. I loved having the attention. I loved feeling like I wasn't on the sidelines anymore, sitting here being practical, logical, straightforward Joan, watching everybody else live their lives. I didn't like it when he called me Joanie, but I didn't want him to stop either." She wiped her face again. "Does that make sense?"

Priscilla nodded, her heart aching for her cousin. "Everybody likes to feel loved. Everybody likes to feel special to at least one other person. Why should you be any different?"

"Because everybody isn't stupid enough to almost get killed for believing what a big fat liar tells her when everyone else is telling her to watch out."

"Calvin isn't that fat," Priscilla said solemnly.

Joan stared at her, and a little smile tickled one corner of her mouth. Then, tears streaming down her face, she started to laugh. Priscilla gave her a fresh tissue to replace the one she had soaked and hugged her again.

"It's all right. Cry all you want to."

Joan drew a hard breath and put on a determined smile. "I'm all right. Thank God nothing more happened to me than a little humiliation. It could have been so much worse."

"I know, but it wasn't. I'm so glad it wasn't. But what happened on the yacht? I was terrified you'd end up in Cuba or South America or just dumped in the ocean somewhere."

"So was I," Joan admitted, blotting her face again. "I was so scared. Calvin told me to sit down and not move unless I wanted him to shoot me, so I did what he told me. He put the gun next to him by the ship's wheel, but he made sure to keep himself between it and me. I didn't have a chance to get it from him. We hadn't gone very far when I saw something move near the door of the bedroom where he kept the cargo he brought in. It was Alessandra. I told Calvin I saw a cutter out the window and said it must be the Coast Guard. While he was looking and telling me not to try anything, she sneaked up on him from the other side, got the gun, and made him turn back to the dock. I've never been so scared in all my life."

"I'm glad you're all right."

"I wasn't that afraid when it was all happening, but afterward, when I realized what might have happened..." There was a tremor in Joan's voice. "I'm sorry I didn't listen to you in the first place."

"I wasn't even sure myself," Priscilla admitted. "I didn't have much more than a feeling that something was wrong. He certainly told some convincing stories, especially that one about Guadalupe. He had to have come up with that one off the top of his head while we were all sitting there."

"He must have," Joan said. "He couldn't have known we would ask about Guadalupe or whether we would know it was a place and not a person. Whatever else he is, he's sure smart."

"Not smart enough to stay on the right side of the law, though you're right about him being quick on his feet. Since that story about poor Guadalupe being killed and how guilty he's felt about that for the past twenty years was something he made up out of whole cloth, I have to wonder what else he's made up."

"Everything," Joan said glumly.

"That story about Justin Weir makes me wonder. If that's a lie too, just how does he fit in to all this?"

Someone knocked on Joan's door. Joan and Priscilla both got up to answer it with Sister at their heels. Standing on the porch, his ponytail sticking out from under a knitted cap, was Justin Weir himself.

"Hey, Priscilla. I didn't expect to see you here." He nodded toward Joan. "I guess you must be Mrs. Abernathy."

Joan narrowed her eyes at him. "What do you want?"

"My name is Justin Weir. May I come in for a moment?"

"What do you want?" Joan repeated, not budging an inch.

He glanced at Priscilla. "Your cousin and I have met before. I heard you had some, uh, difficulties a little while ago, and I thought I'd get the story."

"The story?"

"I saw Mallory, or I guess it's Gallico, get arrested a little while ago. There was no use trying to get anything from him or anyone else involved at that point, so I thought I'd get the inside scoop from you while it's still fresh. Could I come in? Please?" He gave them both a crooked smile. "No use heating the whole neighborhood, right?"

Joan glared at him. "I'm exactly the person you don't want to try anything with today, understand?"

He nodded solemnly, and the women stepped back to let him in.

"So what are you trying to tell us?" Priscilla asked. "You're some kind of reporter?"

"A journalist really." He went over to the fire to warm his hands. He shrugged. "Not actually an art collector."

Joan crossed her arms over her chest. "Not the son of a drug lord's lieutenant bent on avenging his father's death?"

That startled a laugh out of the visitor. "Not that I know of. Who told you that?"

"Never mind," Priscilla said. "Why don't you tell us who you actually are?"

"I really am a journalist." He took out his wallet and showed them a press pass identifying him as an employee of one of the big New York magazines. "You can call my mom too, if you want."

Priscilla couldn't help smiling.

Joan wasn't so easily convinced. "And what are you doing here?"

"Actually, I followed Alessandra Alvarez up here from Peru. I suppose you know who she is by now. She wouldn't give me an interview about tracking down stolen artifacts because she said I'd give her away, but she couldn't keep me from following her up here. I tried to stay out of her way so I wouldn't scare anybody off, but I wanted to see what I could find too."

"In Rayne Forster's studio, for example?" Joan asked.

"Yeah, well." Justin laughed faintly. "The police asked me about that, and I'll be honest. I did tape her back door, but when I went in to look around that night, all the crates that had come from the *Barrett* were gone. I had a quick look around, never touched anything, and then took off. The police didn't have anything on me really, except that I'd been in the gallery that day, and since nothing was damaged or stolen, they didn't hassle me too much. Just told me to keep out of trouble."

"Did you try to get into the studio earlier by breaking a window?" Priscilla asked.

"What? No! I don't know anything about that." Justin shook his head vehemently.

Priscilla was surprised. There was no one else with a motive to get into the studio. Rayne was right—it must have been the wind or something else that broke the window.

"So you don't have any family connection with somebody in Calvin's past?" Joan asked.

"Never met the guy, actually. All I had was a name and a description. Although the name I had was Greg Mallory. I knew Alessandra was after him, so I followed her and asked around."

Justin shrugged. "I guess that's not nearly as exciting as a family vendetta, but that's the truth of it."

Joan's stiff expression softened. "Would you like to sit down? I was about to make some coffee."

Priscilla gave him an encouraging nod, and he smiled at Joan. "I'd like that very much."

"I suppose the police will be by to question me any time now," Joan said a few minutes later as they all sat with mugs of coffee. "I'll tell you the little bit I know on one condition."

Justin lifted his sandy eyebrows.

"I don't want my real name used," Joan said, "and I don't want you to mention the town. I suppose some people will know it's me anyway, but I'd rather not have it blasted all over the place. Okay?"

"Fair enough. May I record our conversation?"

"I don't want to do that. You can take all the notes you want, but that's all. If that's not good enough, then—"

"No, no, that's fine." Justin grinned and took out a steno pad. "My mom told me this would come in handy in college, and she was right. I use it all the time in my work." He began to write in wide loops and squiggles. "Notes regarding Calvin Gallico, aka Greg Mallory."

"Shorthand," Priscilla said. "I haven't seen that in years."

"I know it too," Joan told the reporter sternly. "So don't think you can pull anything over on me."

Justin glanced up from his notepad with a grin. "Wouldn't dream of it. Now, if you'd just tell me about what happened, from the time you met Calvin and with as much detail as you remember, we'll get this over with."

Joan was just finishing telling him what happened with Calvin and Alessandra on the *Barrett* when her telephone rang. The conversation only lasted a few minutes.

"That was April Brown," she said when she'd ended the call. "She's coming over here to interview me about today. If you're supposed to be staying out of trouble," she told Justin, "you'd better finish up and get going."

"Yeah, you're right." He made a few more notes and then stood up. "I appreciate your giving me your story. I think I have everything I need, but would it be okay if I got your phone number just in case I think of something else?"

Joan looked at him dubiously.

"I promise I won't call unless it's really important."

"I don't see what that would hurt," Priscilla said to Joan. "You can always refuse the call if you want to."

"I guess so." Joan gave him her phone number. "I'm trusting you to keep your word."

"I will." Justin bundled up again, then shook hands with Joan and Priscilla. "Thank you both. I think my editor will be very interested in what happened today. I'll still have to find out what I can about what happens to Gallico, but this will be a big help."

Joan and Sister showed him to the door.

"I hope you have a Merry Christmas," he said as he leaned down to pat Sister's head. "All of you."

Once he was gone, Joan sat on the sofa next to Priscilla and picked up her coffee cup again. "To tell the truth, it made me feel a little better just to talk everything out like that. Not that I don't still feel like an idiot."

"Joan! Did you even listen to yourself a little while ago? Calvin's a con man. He knew exactly what to do to make you feel sorry for him, to make you defend him, to make you trust him. He's very good at it too. You remember how quickly he came up with elaborate backstories for Alessandra and Justin and even Guadalupe, who's not a person at all. Who knows how many other people he's used like this? Look at poor Rayne. He got her to help him sell his illegal goods, and she'd never done anything like that before."

"Rayne was in on it?" Joan bit her lip. "I really am gullible, aren't I? I never would have believed it of her."

"I wouldn't have either, so don't feel bad about that. And, to be honest, I don't think she would've kept it up, once she took time to think it through. Calvin just got to her at a vulnerable time, and she felt desperate."

"Why?" Joan asked. "I thought she had her oh-so-wonderful husband to take care of her."

"That was all a front," Priscilla told her. "He left her for someone else a few months ago, and then she found out that she's expecting a baby."

"Oh." Joan's dubious expression softened into sympathy. "That's a lot to deal with all at once. I can see how Calvin would be able to play on that to get her to help him. Ugh. I just want to kick him all the way back to Peru."

"I'm sure everyone from the police to the Coast Guard to the Peruvian Embassy, not to mention all kinds of federal agencies, will see to him. It may take years for them to even figure out who gets to bring what charges against him. And all that time, he won't be able to take advantage of anyone else."

Joan was silent for a moment, swirling the dregs of her coffee in the bottom of her cup. "I guess I'll have to testify against him too."

"Eventually, yes. For now, I expect you'll just have to make a statement to the police so they can press charges against him and put him in jail. You know how it is with the courts. It may be months before they have an actual trial. But don't worry. Everything's okay."

Joan nodded, head down.

"Relax!" Priscilla took her by the shoulders and forced her to make eye contact. "It's over, and everything's okay."

"It is," Joan said with a determined smile, and then she started to cry again.

CHAPTER NINETEEN

Trudy showed up only a minute or two after Justin left. She immediately wrapped her sister in a huge hug and wouldn't let her go.

"I was so scared! I thought he was going to take you out to sea and shoot you or throw you into the ocean or something!"

"It's all right," Joan said. "Thank you for helping Priscilla get me out of trouble."

Trudy shook her head, platinum curls bobbing. "She did everything. I just tried to distract Rayne, and I didn't even do that very well!"

"It worked out just fine," Priscilla insisted. "We found out what we wanted to know."

"I appreciate you both," Joan said as they all settled on the couch and she situated herself between them. "Tell me what happened after Calvin made me leave Rayne's."

"I called the police and then I called Gerald. He was already out that way, and he said he'd take care of contacting the Coast Guard and all that." Trudy glanced at Priscilla. "I hope you're not mad about me calling him. I just thought he would know what to do."

"I don't quite know what he's been up to, to tell you the truth," Priscilla said, "but he definitely wasn't doing what I thought he was doing."

"What do you mean?" Joan asked.

"Oh, I don't know. I was worried that, with everything that's going on with his family, that he might be taking money to let Calvin do whatever he wanted without the Coast Guard stopping him."

Joan's eyes widened. "Gerald? Are you crazy?"

"Yeah." Priscilla laughed softly. "I guess I am. Still, I know there's something going on with him, but it's not that."

"Then what?" Trudy asked.

"I guess I'll have to wait to find out about that until he and I have a chance to talk."

It didn't take long for the police to come out to Joan's cottage to talk to Joan and Trudy. Trudy was her usual emphatic, excitable self. Joan gave Officer Brown her statement, succinct and without emotion. Even when they were alone again, Joan was only quietly matter of fact.

Gail's arrival with a piping-hot chicken casserole brought a refreshing sense of normalcy with it. Trudy had brought a broccoli, corn, and green bean salad that was a delicious complement to it, and by the time they had eaten dinner and then indulged in the cake Joan had intended to share with Calvin that evening, they'd told Gail about everything that had happened earlier.

"That's what I get for being the only one with a full-time job," Gail grumbled. "I miss out on all the action." She gave Joan a warm smile. "But I'm so glad you're all right."

"Me too. And the next time I act like I don't have any brains, one of you hit me over the head or something."

"We'll just have anyone who wants to go out with you checked out by the FBI first," Trudy said.

Priscilla was glad to hear Joan laugh at that, glad to see she wasn't too upset. It was going to be hard enough to forgive Calvin for taking advantage of her, for toying with her heart and then crushing it underfoot when he didn't need her anymore, but it would have been almost impossible to forgive him if he had made her really fall in love with him. She was actually glad when Joan turned down her offer to stay the night. She turned down Trudy's and Gail's too. Calvin had hurt her, but he hadn't broken her. Her bruises would heal, and she would be fine.

It was getting late when Priscilla finally got home and took Jake for a quick walk, but she made a cup of tea and called Gerald anyway.

"I hope it's not too late," she said when he answered.

"Not at all. How's Joan doing?"

"She's all right." Priscilla sat at the kitchen table with Jake at her feet and let the tea warm her from the inside out. "I know she'll need some time, but I think she'll be fine."

"Good." Gerald didn't say anything for a moment, and then he cleared his throat. "Look, I know it's a little late, but we need to talk. Could I come over for a few minutes? I'd rather not do this over the phone."

"Uh, sure. It's not that late anyway. Just a little after nine."

"Good. I'll be right there."

He was as good as his word. He always was.

"You wouldn't happen to have another cup of that tea I smell, would you?" he asked after he had taken off his coat and gloves and warmed himself for a minute by the fire. "I always need a warm-up this time of year."

"Why don't we sit in the kitchen? It's pretty cozy in there even without a fireplace."

He nodded and followed her to the table. It took only a minute for her to pour him a cup of her favorite blend and refresh hers.

She put his cup on the table in front of him. "Listen, Gerald, I feel terrible about suspecting you. I can't believe I actually thought you would do something illegal. The only excuse I have is that I was so worried about Joan, and you were too, and then it felt like you weren't anymore, and I couldn't figure out why. Then there was the whole 'I'd do anything to help my family…'"

She sat down across from him, warming her hands around her own cup, unable to look him in the eye. "I know the kind of man you are, and I trust you to do what's right." She shook her head. "I guess I was just so upset about what was going on with Joan and seeing suspicious activity everywhere."

"You didn't really think I was taking a payoff, did you? Really?"

She shrugged. "I wasn't sure what to think. When you told me to keep out of the business and then when I saw you take money from that man on the beach—"

"Yes, you said that before. What you saw didn't have anything to do with Calvin or the smuggling."

"But that man gave you a huge roll of bills. I saw him."

Gerald shook his head. "You saw him *offer* me a huge roll of bills, but you couldn't have seen me take it, because I didn't."

Priscilla thought for a moment. What had she actually seen? The man had taken out the money, and then that van had driven by and blocked her view. After that, she had seen Gerald shaking the man's hand. Didn't that mean they had made some kind of deal?

"You didn't?"

"Nope," Gerald said. "It was a fair amount of money, I'll grant you, but not what I was asking for the *Aggie Jean*."

Priscilla gaped at him. "Wait. What? You aren't selling your boat are you? You can't!"

"Actually, I can. And, actually, I will. As soon as I get a decent price for her."

"Oh, Gerald, no. You love that boat. It's the *Aggie Jean*!"

"See? That's why I didn't tell you what I had in mind. I know Aggie will throw a fit when she finds out about it, and that's why I'm not telling her anything until it's a done deal."

Priscilla exhaled. "You don't know how relieved I am now."

Gerald's forehead wrinkled. "Relieved?"

"This guy must be the one Aggie was worried about."

"What do you mean?"

"She called me a few days back and told me she was worried about what you were going to do to raise some money to help them with the medical bills. She was afraid you were going to do something dangerous, something crazy, to get it. She said you were at her house when you got a call that you stepped outside to take, and when she asked you about it you said it was 'just a guy' and wouldn't tell her anything else."

"Oh, yeah. Yeah, that was Rico. He wants to buy the boat, but he's only got about two-thirds of my asking price. He said he could pay me in cash if I'd cut him a deal. I turned him down, and he got the money out to show me he wasn't kidding. I still turned him down, but I told him I might call him back later if I didn't get a better offer. He said he'd see if he could come up with a little more money in the meantime. So we shook on it, and that was that."

"And that's what made me wonder even more if you weren't taking bribes."

"Even more?"

"Yeah, well, uh . . . " She knew her face was beet red now. "I saw you talking to Alessandra. You weren't in uniform, even though you told me you were at work, and you were both in the shadows, like you didn't want to be seen. That and you telling me to stay out of Calvin's business, it just made me wonder."

"And assume." He shook his head. "If you want to know the truth, yes, I was actually working that day. She wanted us to know what she suspected about Calvin so we could keep an eye on him. Obviously she couldn't be seen talking to a Coast Guard captain, and she couldn't come to the station, so we had a quick talk there and I wasn't in uniform. Make sense now?"

She nodded. "I'm sorry. I'm really, really sorry."

He reached across the table to take her hand. "I know you were concerned about Joan. You don't have to keep apologizing."

He shook his head, grinning at her. "Seriously. You thought I was skulking around taking bribes on the beach?"

"Well, in my defense, if it had been just for the money, I would never have believed it of you, but I know how worried you are about having enough to pay for Ava's treatment. I know even a good man can be driven to do something desperate if he thinks he has to."

"I hope I'm never so desperate that I do something like that." He gave her that lopsided grin again. "Selling the *Aggie Jean* is as far as I hope I ever have to go."

"Are you sure you have to sell her?"

"I've been praying God will provide for us, but this is all I can come up with." He squeezed her hand and released it. "It's all right. It's just a boat."

There was a flicker of regret in his eyes, but it was gone as quickly as it had come.

"Don't do anything just yet," she said. "At least wait until after Christmas."

"Why? Nothing's going to change."

"It might. Besides, what will a few more days hurt?"

"Priscilla—"

"Is there any reason you have to have the money this minute? The doctors haven't even done anything yet. They won't until after New Year's."

He frowned. "It's not like somebody's going to give me a wad of cash for Christmas you know. And I have a willing buyer now."

"But he might be able to give you a little more for the boat later, if it even comes down to that after all."

He let out a slow breath.

"Just a few days more," she said. "For me."

"For you."

There was a glint of humor in his eye. And maybe, just maybe, there was something more.

"Thanks for understanding," she said, busying herself with the string on her teabag. "Uh, would you like more?"

He looked regretfully into his cup and shook his head. "Really, I ought to get home now. It's getting late, and besides, it's getting really cold again, and Sammy will wonder where I am."

He stood up, and she walked with him to the door.

"Thanks for coming by," she said.

"I'm glad we could clear all this up." He put on his coat and gloves and hat. "And I'm glad Joan's okay."

"Oh, me too." Priscilla shuddered. "It could have been so much worse."

"Good thing we were all looking out for her." Gerald gave her a quick, comforting hug. "And God was looking out for all of us."

"I know," she murmured, ducking her head against his shoulder. "I know."

"I'll call you," he said, squeezing her once again before he released her. "Have a good night's sleep."

"You too."

She watched as he got into his SUV and drove away. Then she shut the door and went back to the warmth of the fire, wishing he were still there to share it with her.

CHAPTER TWENTY

Over the next few days, the bustle of preparing for Christmas was compounded by the ensuing fallout from Calvin's smuggling attempts. Rayne was arrested for her part in the operation, but she was quickly released on bail. Because of her cooperation with the police, her ready admission of guilt, and her agreement to testify against Calvin when he came to trial, her court-appointed attorney had great hopes that the judge in her own trial would be lenient. Her impending motherhood and her previous lack of criminal record were elements in her favor too.

Priscilla asked about her when April Brown requested that she come back to the police station to clear up one more matter in the smuggling case.

"Rayne's doing well," April said once they were settled at a small round table in a conference room. "She's not off the hook by any means, but I have a feeling she'll get through this all right. She doesn't seem like the type to be a career criminal."

"Unlike Calvin."

"Yeah. I'll tell you what, I've seen a lot of crooks in my time, but that guy is something else. He spins excuses out of thin air like cotton candy."

"I know. He's good, isn't he?"

"A real pro. No wonder your cousin believed him. Among others."

"Others?"

"Yeah," April said. "Mr. and Mrs. Graham were shocked to know what he was using their dock for, but there really wasn't any way for them to know what he was up to."

"So what am I here for this time?" Priscilla asked. "I think I've told you everything I know."

"Actually, there's someone else we're waiting for—"

"Hey, Priscilla."

Her whole inside turned warm at the sound of Gerald's voice, and she turned to see him smiling at her from the door of the conference room, his Coast Guard hat in his hands and that unruly lock of dark hair falling down over his forehead.

"What are you doing here?" she asked as he took the seat beside her.

"Something about the Gallico case. What about you?"

"Same thing."

"Actually," April said, "while this is related to the case, there's someone else who'd like to talk to you both." She picked up the phone and pushed a button. "Send her in."

A moment later, Alessandra Alvarez strode into the room wearing a black silk skirt and jacket with a blouse and spike heels in that particular shade of orange known as Tiger Lily. Her shining black hair was pulled into a low bun at the back of her neck. As always, she looked absolutely professional and absolutely stunning.

"I'm glad you both could come," she said, seating herself once they all shook hands. "And thank you, Officer Brown, for arranging this meeting."

"I'm happy to do it," April said. "Though I feel like this is something an ambassador or someone like that should be doing."

Priscilla glanced at Gerald, but he looked as puzzled as she felt.

"No," Alessandra said with a light laugh. "Although our government may eventually send a letter of commendation or something of that sort, at present I am here to let you know that we are not ungrateful for what these two have done to help return our artifacts to their rightful place and to catch and prosecute the man responsible for taking them out of the country." She turned to Gerald. "Captain O'Bannon—"

"Well, I was only doing my duty," Gerald began, but Alessandra shook her head.

"From what I understand, you did far more, but because of your position in the Coast Guard, I am afraid all I can offer you is my country's thanks."

He gave her a rueful smile. "That was what I was about to say. I can't take any reward for just doing my job."

"Exactly so, which is why it is my pleasure to present the entire reward to Mrs. Grant."

"Reward?" Priscilla stared at her. "There's a reward?"

Alessandra nodded, her dark eyes sparkling. "There is, Mrs. Grant. Our government has been trying to stop these thefts and retrieve these items for many years now, and I've been working with your local police as well as your federal government to keep the contraband from coming into the States. Arresting Calvin Gallico and tracking down those to whom he sold our artifacts will be a major step in that direction. He's just the tip of the iceberg, of course, but now that we have him, we should be able to identify many others working with him, both in our country and in yours."

Gerald nodded in encouragement. "Sometimes it takes just one good collar to bust a whole ring wide open. If you hadn't been so sure something was going on with him and Joan, he might never have been caught."

The admiration in his eyes warmed Priscilla all over. "I was mostly just worried about my cousin," she said.

"But you refused to give up, even when things became difficult," Alessandra said. "Tenacity is a good quality to have."

"Some people call it stubbornness," Priscilla admitted, and Gerald chuckled.

"Whatever it is, we appreciate it." Alessandra took a paper from her handbag and slid it across the table to her. "As you can see."

The letterhead was from some agency in Peru, though since it was in Spanish, Priscilla couldn't tell which one. But the text of the letter was in English. Her eyes widened as she read it, especially when she came to the amount of the reward.

"You're kidding, right?"

Alessandra shook her head.

"But that's in pesos, isn't it?"

"Peru uses soles, not pesos," Gerald said.

Priscilla felt her face warm. "I'm sorry. I'm not familiar with South American currency."

"It's not a problem," Alessandra said, her smile warm. "But no, that is not soles. That is American dollars."

"But—" Shaking her head, Priscilla passed the letter to Gerald.

He whistled under his breath. "That's a nice reward. Congratulations."

"But I can't really take that, can I?"

"We hope you do," Alessandra said. "What we will be able to recover because of you, in money and in importance to our culture, is worth many times more." She looked significantly at Gerald. "Once you have accepted it, Mrs. Grant, it is, of course, yours to do with as you please."

"I see." Priscilla had to force herself not to grin like an idiot. "Then, yes, I would be very happy to accept. And thank you."

The days leading up to Christmas Eve went quickly. Priscilla barely had time to finish her preparations before it was time to go to Trudy's for the party. Her large, airy living room boasted an enormous Christmas tree with twinkling lights and a stack of presents beneath. It was also full of people, mostly family, but Priscilla was glad to see that Rayne had also been invited.

"Joan's idea," Trudy whispered while they were still at the door. "But I wish I had thought of it first. She was so happy to come."

Priscilla gave her a huge hug. "That's wonderful."

Once she had said hello to everyone she knew and been introduced to the few she didn't, Priscilla deposited her own stack of presents under the tree and then went to where Rayne was sitting, mostly observing everyone else.

"I'm glad you could come, Rayne. I was afraid you'd be by yourself tonight."

"Your cousins have been so sweet." Rayne's smile was a little wistful, but she did seem happy to be there. "I didn't bring any presents, but I made fudge for everyone."

"That's perfect! Just don't tell anyone until after dinner. Otherwise nobody will eat anything else."

Rayne laughed softly, and then she sighed. "I'm so sorry about everything. I just—"

"It's all right," Priscilla said, shushing her. "It's Christmas, a time for forgiveness and thanksgiving and knowing how much God loves us and wants us to be reconciled to Him and to each other." She nodded toward the old-fashioned nativity that was displayed on a little table near the tree. "That's what Christmas is all about."

Rayne bit her lip. "I know. I've gotten away from all that, but I know. Thanks for reminding me." She put one hand on her barely rounded stomach. "I think we're going to be all right."

Priscilla hugged her. Before they could say anything else, Rachel and A.J. came in from the cold, and Priscilla went to hug them both and then took them around to meet everyone. It took her a few minutes to realize that she hadn't seen Joan anywhere yet.

"Where's Joan?" she asked Gail once she had exchanged hugs with her and Uncle Hugh.

"You know how she is," Uncle Hugh said. "Always bustling around doing something."

"She's been keeping out of sight," Gail said once her father had wandered off to talk to Trudy's husband about where he'd gotten the tree. "Trudy did most of the cooking, but Joan's been in the kitchen keeping things simmering. She doesn't want anyone asking her about Calvin and all that."

"Oh, surely no one would," Priscilla said, glancing around the cozy, people-filled room. "Not tonight."

"I think she's just a little embarrassed. You know."

"I'll go talk to her."

Priscilla went into the kitchen and found Joan basting a perfectly browned turkey.

"Ooh, delicious." Priscilla hugged her. "Merry Christmas!"

"Merry Christmas to you." Joan hugged her back, clinging just a moment longer after Priscilla released her. "I'm glad you're here."

Priscilla gave her an understanding smile. "How's it going?"

"Oh, fine."

Priscilla wasn't convinced.

Joan sighed. "Everybody out there seems to have someone. Even Gail's been talking to Tommy Townsend most of the evening. I just wish…" She ended with a vague shake of her head.

"You're not missing Calvin, are you?"

"No!" Joan shook her head. "Not him, not at all. But on nights like this it would be nice to have someone special, you know?"

Priscilla leaned against the counter. "Your boys are still coming, aren't they?"

"They are." Joan perked up a little at that. "They called to say they were running late, but they're still coming. But maybe until they get here you and I could stick together?"

She didn't have to say anything more. Priscilla understood. And she'd be happy to stay with Joan until whatever awkwardness she was feeling wore off. And, knowing the rest of the family, it would wear off soon.

"That would be great," Priscilla told her. "And we can try to guess what's in all the presents."

"I'm so glad you ended up staying here with us," Joan said, her somber expression unchanged. "I don't know what I'd do without you."

"And I don't know what I'd do without you. Together we're unstoppable, right?"

For just a second or two, Priscilla wondered if her cousin was going to answer her. Then Joan lifted her head and smiled. "You know, you're absolutely right. Let me just put this back into the oven, and we can enjoy some of our famous family wassail."

The mixture of citrus, brown sugar, and cinnamon filled the whole house with the smell of Christmas, and it was always a special moment when everyone toasted the season. Since he and Trudy were the hosts again, Dan was the one to raise the customary toast.

"To Christmas," he said, lifting his cup. "May we never take this season or each other for granted."

"To Christmas," everyone echoed, and then they drank.

"Time for dinner, everyone," Trudy said. "Thanks to Joan, everything ought to be just perfect."

"Trudy's the cook," Joan told everybody. "I just did a little stirring."

"Joan made the gravy," Trudy said.

"And she makes the best," Uncle Hugh added.

A number of voices were lifted in agreement, and Joan shook her head, waving one hand dismissively. Priscilla could tell, though, that the affirmation had pleased her. It was only a small thing, but it was just what Joan needed.

Dinner was delicious, of course, especially Joan's gravy, and as soon as it was over, everyone gathered by the Christmas tree to open presents. They were mostly little things, some practical, some nostalgic, some humorous, but it was fun to see each of them unwrapped, and the pleasure each gave to the recipient and to the giver.

It seemed like forever, and Priscilla didn't know how it ended up being the very last package for the evening, but Joan finally got to open the gift Priscilla had brought for her.

Joan shook the box before she tore off the paper. "Hmmmm. I don't hear any jingle bells or anything."

Trudy laughed. "Remember how Mom used to put ball bearings and other little rattling things in our packages so we couldn't guess what they were?"

"Exactly." Joan gave Priscilla an arched glance. "I guess I'll just have to open it." But when she did, her smile faded. "Oh, my."

"What is it?" Uncle Hugh demanded. "Show us."

"You can't have seen much of it yet," Rachel said, grinning up at A.J. and then over at Priscilla. Of course, Rachel knew exactly what it was. Priscilla had sent her photos of just about every step she took to make it.

"Oh, Priscilla," Joan breathed, lifting the quilt from the box. "You didn't."

"I've been wanting to make one for you just forever," Priscilla said.

Joan hugged it close, still folded. "I love it."

"You haven't seen anything but the back," Trudy said.

Joan stroked the soft pink-and-green floral print. "But it's wonderful."

"You still might want to look at the front," Priscilla said. "That's where all the pretty is."

Joan laughed. "I already know it's gorgeous."

She hugged the quilt one more time and then carefully unfolded it, revealing a profusion of delicately appliquéd flowers.

"Oh, my," she breathed again, shaking her head. "Priscilla, you're amazing. It's my garden. It's just like my garden."

One of the highlights of Joan's cottage was the lovely English country garden she maintained. Priscilla had reproduced it, trellises and all, as best she was able.

"I thought you'd like to have it blooming in the winter as well as in the summer."

"Thank you."

Joan passed the quilt off to Trudy and the others eager to examine it up close and went to Priscilla.

"It's wonderful." She hugged Priscilla tightly. "You're wonderful."

"I was afraid I wouldn't get it done in time, but I'm so glad I did. I wanted to do something to let you know how special you are to me." Priscilla squeezed both of her hands. "And how much I love you."

Tears sparkled in Joan's eyes, but she was smiling too. "Thank you. Thank you for taking care of me even when I didn't think I needed you to."

Priscilla hugged her again. "What are cousins for?"

"Joan!" Gail called. "Did you see these hollyhocks? They look like the real thing."

Joan gave Priscilla's hand a final clasp and then went back to look at her quilt. Priscilla let out a deep breath. No matter how many quilts she made and gave away, she was always worried that someone she gave one to wouldn't like it. She never should have worried.

"That is a wonderfully thoughtful gift."

Surprised to hear Gerald's voice behind her, Priscilla turned. "When did you get here?"

"Dan let me in a few minutes ago. I got to see the last of the presents being opened." He smiled into her eyes. "She's right, you know. You're amazing."

"It's not much." Okay, that wasn't quite true. It had actually been a lot of work, but what else was she supposed to say?

"It's a beautiful quilt," he said, "but that's not what I was talking about."

Now she really didn't know what to say. "Uh, I have a present for you, but I wasn't sure you'd be here, so I left it in the car."

"That's all right." His hazel eyes crinkled at the corners. "But I have something for you."

He led her into the dining room and slid a large, flat package from behind the china cabinet. It was wrapped in shiny blue paper with white snowflakes on it and tied with a red ribbon.

"What is it?" she asked.

"You'll have to open it and see."

She looked at the package for a moment. "Maybe I'd better get yours first."

"That can wait. Really. Just open it."

"Okay." She couldn't help the little tremor in her voice.

She slipped her finger under each place where the paper was taped, and quickly had it off. Then she peeled a strip of shipping tape off the box inside and opened the flaps. There smiling up at her, perfectly framed and matted, were Trudy, Gail, Joan, and herself.

"You sneak!"

Grinning, he held the box as she lifted the picture out of it.

"This is one of the pictures you took at Thanksgiving," she said. "When you were 'just trying out the new camera.' I totally forgot about it. Look at this. You managed to get a good shot of all of us at the same time."

"Whew." He wiped imaginary sweat from his forehead. "I was hoping you'd say that. I know how picky people can be about their pictures."

"No, it's perfect. Really, really perfect."

Truly it was. Joan was sitting on the couch with Priscilla at her right and Gail at her left. Trudy was snuggled next to Gail. Priscilla was leaning over to have her face next to Joan's, and Trudy and Gail were leaning in too, so all four of them were nearly cheek to cheek. They looked as if they had just been laughing, and their eyes were bright with joy and warm with love.

She tried to tell Gerald again how perfect it was, but somehow the words couldn't get past the tightness in her throat.

"I'm glad you like it," he said softly, understanding.

"What a beautiful mat and frame," she managed finally, and she stroked one finger down the antique-white frame, her own reflection smiling back at her from the gleaming glass that covered the picture and the soft yellow mat that set it off. "It'll go beautifully with everything in my living room."

"I thought you'd like it," Gerald said. "I wanted to give you something special, and I know how close you and your cousins have become. How important family is to you."

She gave him a hug. "I know it's important to you too. I thought you'd want to spend the evening with Aggie and the kids."

"I did already. We had dinner together, and by then the little ones were ready for bed. Aggie said she and Nick would have their hands full getting ready for Santa, and they sent me over here to relax a little."

"I'm glad they did. I knew Trudy had asked you, but I wasn't sure if you'd come."

"Sure," he said. "I wouldn't miss it. And I wanted to give you this." He shrugged a little. "I know it's nothing compared to what you did for Aggie and the baby. For what you did for me."

"It wasn't me," she said softly. She looked down at the picture again. "Not much anyway. I just wanted Joan to be safe. That reward money was a miracle. I know it was. And you deserved at least half of it. I'm not going to argue with God's way of providing for what your family needed, and I don't think you should either."

She gave him a challenging look, and he laughed.

"Well, if you put it that way, I guess there's not much I can do but accept it and be thankful. And I am." He looked deeply into her eyes. "Thankful for everything God has provided for me."

He took the picture from her, put it back into the box, and put the box on the table. Then he took her arm and walked her over to the place where the dining room opened into the kitchen. Her pulse beat a little faster when she saw someone had hung up a red-ribboned cluster of mistletoe, and she and Gerald were standing right underneath it.

"I can't thank you enough for what you did for Ava and for all of us," he said, catching her hand in his before she could step away.

She could feel a touch of warmth in her cheeks. It was more than just the effect of the fireplace and a house full of people.

"It was only right," she murmured. "You did most of the work, most of the dangerous part anyway, and it's not fair that you shouldn't have gotten any of the reward. Besides, God has blessed me more than I could even imagine. It's only right that I should share at least a little of that with people who need it. People I care about."

She squeezed his hand, and his hold tightened just the slightest bit.

"He's blessed me too," Gerald said, his voice low and tender. "Aggie and the kids, a job that makes a difference." His mouth turned up at one side. "People *I* care about."

He leaned closer and, seemingly of their own accord, her eyes fluttered closed. The touch of his lips on hers was brief, but it sent a delicious warmth all through her. When she opened her eyes again, he was smiling at her.

"I hear Seth's Pond is frozen again, and it's awfully romantic skating out there in the moonlight."

"So I've heard," she murmured.

Gerald winked at her. "Merry Christmas, Priscilla."

She felt her heart turn over with the thought of what could be in their future. "Merry Christmas, Gerald. And may God bless us, every one."

AUTHOR LETTER

Dear Reader,

Don't you love Christmas? I know I do.

Yes, it can be stressful trying to make everything, buy everything, cook everything, decorate everything, visit everything, and do everything. It can be hard to make plans that work for everyone, especially with extended and blended families, and especially if those plans have to change at the last minute. It can be exhausting just trying to keep everything straight, and when you're concerned about someone you love, it can be even more difficult.

But even in the midst of the chaos and stress, Christmas is still a beautiful time. Whether they acknowledge it or not, the whole world stops in honor of the birth of Jesus Christ, God's perfect gift to all His creation. All we really have to do is thank Him.

God bless us, every one!
DeAnna Julie Dodson

ABOUT THE AUTHOR

DeAnna Julie Dodson has always been an avid reader and a lover of storytelling, whether on the page, the screen, or the stage. This, along with her keen interest in history and her Christian faith, shows in her many published books about love, forgiveness, and triumph over adversity. A fifth-generation Texan, she makes her home north of Dallas with three spoiled cats and, when not writing, spends her free time quilting, cross-stitching, and watching NHL hockey.

AN ARMCHAIR TOUR OF
MARTHA'S VINEYARD
Ice-skating on Uncle Seth's Pond

Uncle Seth's Pond, one of only two freshwater ponds on Martha's Vineyard, is located off Lamberts Cove Road in West Tisbury. It's busy, along with the rest of the island, during the summer season, but what about in the winter? Martha's Vineyard is surrounded by the ocean, and the December temperatures are frequently above freezing. But when it happens to get cold enough long enough, the excitement passes from person to person. The pond is frozen! Time for ice-skating!

A pond that is usually just slush during the winter is suddenly the perfect sunny-day venue for ice-skating or even a game of pick-up hockey. People who generally like to walk or jog for exercise become skaters, enjoying the Christmassy feel of the ice and snow and the fresh holiday wind in their faces and the adventure of gliding across the frozen water. And, in the twilight or under the moon and stars, the frozen pond becomes a romantic picture postcard, a delightful break in the midst of the long, housebound winter.

Although a hard freeze will transform any thick pool of water into an ice rink, Uncle Seth's Pond is considered one of the finest. Just make sure the ice is safe for skating!

SOMETHING DELICIOUS FROM OUR SEASIDE FRIENDS

Priscilla's Delicious Lane Cake

Ingredients:

2 boxes white cake mix

1 teaspoon almond extract

1 teaspoon vanilla extract

For Frosting:

12 egg yolks

1½ cups sugar

2 cups butter

2 tablespoons plus
  2 teaspoons vanilla
  extract

⅓ cup apple juice or orange
  juice

1 teaspoon almond extract

2 cups raisins

2 cups chopped pecans

2 cups shredded coconut

Directions:

Prepare cake mix according to package directions and add vanilla and almond extract. Pour into four round cake pans, bake, and allow to cool.

For frosting, mix egg yolks and sugar in a double boiler over simmering water. Stir constantly until mixture is smooth and light colored. Add a few tablespoons butter at a time, stirring constantly, until mixture thickens and is almost see-through. Remove pan from heat and stir in vanilla and almond extracts and juice. Add raisins, pecans, and coconut. Allow mixture to cool enough to spread easily, usually about 10 minutes, before frosting the cake.

Note: The frosting is usually made with bourbon, but I prefer this modified version.

Read on for a sneak peek of the first book in
an exciting new mystery series from
Guideposts Books—Whistle Stop Café Mysteries!

Under the Apple Tree
by Gabrielle Meyer

Dust motes floated on the warm, thick air as Debbie Albright shoved a cardboard box into the corner of her attic. A sneeze started to build in her nose, forcing her to stop what she was doing and hold her hand above her lip. Her eyes watered, but the feeling soon passed.

"Your allergies will never survive this move." Janet Shaw, Debbie's best friend, tossed her a box of tissues. "Should we take a break? The coffee shop has half-priced mochas on Saturdays."

Debbie pulled a tissue free. "We don't have time for a break. I want to get all the storage boxes out of the living room before Ian gets here with the furniture." He would be arriving any minute, and Debbie and Janet still had several more trips to make up the two flights of stairs to the attic.

The air was hot and stuffy, and a hundred years' worth of dust lined the cracks and crevices of the old shiplap on the ceiling and walls. Beneath her feet, the boards creaked in protest, reminding Debbie that the home was old and she had a big job ahead of her. But she couldn't be happier or more excited to finally be back in Dennison, Ohio. The beautiful craftsman-style bungalow she had purchased would need quite a bit of work, but she wasn't afraid to tackle the project, especially with her friends' help.

"It looks like Mr. Zink left a few treasures for you," Janet commented. The lid on an old trunk creaked in protest as she lifted it.

"He mentioned that his nieces and nephews left a few odds and ends." Debbie shoved the used tissue into the pocket of her overalls as she moved around several boxes to join Janet. "But he said most of it would probably need to be thrown away."

"This looks like it's full of old newspapers." Janet bent down and lifted one from the trunk, her blue eyes opening wide. "This is from December 1941."

Debbie took the paper from Janet and slipped one of her brown curls back into the bandanna tied around her head. Despite the heat, a chill climbed up her spine as she read the headline. "'War Declared.'" Even though it had happened before her lifetime, she still felt a keen tug in her heart when she thought about World War II. "I can't even imagine what it would have been like to live through such a difficult time."

Janet lifted more newspapers out of the trunk. "Some of these are from the *Dennison Daily Transcript* and talk about all the troops coming through the depot."

"I could read these for hours."

Janet stood up straight. "We'll have to go through all this later."

"I probably won't have much free time, even after I'm settled." Not with all the work she had to do on the house and the plans they had to open the Whistle Stop Café in the old train depot a few blocks up the street. After leaving her corporate job in Cleveland, Debbie had come back to town to do just that. Somehow, she'd convinced Janet to help her, knowing what an amazing cook and baker her best friend had become over the years. Janet had worked for the Third Street Bakery for much of her career and was ready to start her own business. Their grand opening would be in three weeks, which meant they still had a massive amount of work ahead of them.

As Debbie lowered the newspaper back into the trunk, something else caught her attention. "What's this?"

An olive-green metal box with the stenciled words SPECIAL SERVICES, US ARMY sat at the bottom of the trunk. Leather straps on the sides made it easy for Debbie to lift out, but they were stiff and cracked with age. She was afraid they would break.

Janet watched as Debbie set the metal box on the dusty floor.

"It's definitely military issue, whatever it is." Debbie ran her fingers along the stenciled words. Iron-clad corner protectors and rivets lined the seams, while clasps held the top and bottom together. "And it's old," she added.

"I bet it's from the 1940s, like the newspapers." Janet squatted next to Debbie. "Do you think it belonged to Mr. Zink?"

"I'm sure it did. He was an infantryman during the war. He fought in Europe and came home to tell about it."

"Do you think he meant to leave it when he moved?" Janet leaned over to inspect the side of the box.

"I don't know." Debbie unhooked the clasps and gently pulled upwards. The hinges groaned, but the box held a wonderful surprise. "It's a portable phonograph!"

"I didn't even know there was such a thing way back then."

The phonograph was in great shape for its age. "Who would ever guess that such an ugly box could house such a beautiful instrument?"

"Do you know how it works?"

Debbie had seen one similar to it in an antique store once, and the owner had shown her how it worked, but the one she'd seen had been in a lot worse shape. "If I remember correctly…" She lifted a handle from the bottom left-hand corner and inserted it into the front of the box. It was curved, and she used it to crank the mechanism. When it was tight, she reached up and shifted a lever, and the turntable began to spin.

"Amazing!" Janet's voice held awe. "I can't believe it still works."

"These things are worth a lot of money," Debbie said. "I need to let Mr. Zink know he forgot to take it."

"Do you think maybe…" Janet rose and went back to the trunk where she moved the rest of the newspapers. "Bingo!" She lifted a thin cardboard sheath.

Debbie smiled as she took the small record. The label in the center had a handwritten note on it, which she read out loud. "'To Ray, with love, Eleanor.'" Under that was the song title, "Don't Sit Under the Apple Tree (With Anyone Else but Me)."

Janet stared at the record. "Do you think Ray is Mr. Zink?"

Debbie nodded. "His first name is Raymond." She flipped off the turntable and let it come to a stop and then set the record on it before pushing the lever again. Her heart pounded as she lifted the needle and gently set it on the record, hoping she knew what she was doing. The last thing she wanted to do was damage the record or the phonograph.

The noise was scratchy at first, and then a clear, beautiful voice filled the attic, singing a version of the Andrews Sisters' popular song.

Debbie looked up and met Janet's surprised gaze. "Who do you think Eleanor was?"

"Whoever she was, she had a great voice."

"This sounds like an amateur recording," Debbie said. "I wonder if she was Mr. Zink's sweetheart."

"He never got married, did he?" Janet asked. "I wonder what happened to Eleanor."

Debbie perked up when she heard a noise from downstairs. "It sounds like Ian is here."

Janet sighed. "I was hoping we could listen to the other records in the trunk." She shrugged. "There'll be time later, I suppose."

Debbie lifted the needle and switched off the turntable. As Janet rose and went to the stairs to greet her husband, Debbie gently slid the record back into its sheath.

Mr. Zink must have forgotten that the phonograph and records were in the attic. It didn't seem right to keep them from him. As soon as she had a bit of free time, she'd stop by the assisted-living home and ask him what he wanted her to do with the trunk.

It would give her a chance to visit with the elderly man again and give him an update on her big move. He'd always been one of her favorite people, full of fun stories and interesting historical tidbits about Dennison. She would take any excuse she could find to stop in and visit.

The portable phonograph, not to mention Eleanor's record, was the perfect reason.

The next day, Debbie had a few minutes after church to stop in and visit Raymond Zink. He had moved into the Good Shepherd Assisted Living Home a couple of months earlier, after deciding to sell his home to Debbie. She was familiar with the Good Shepherd, since her dad had recently retired from managing the facility.

Debbie passed through the front doors and into the cozy foyer. The sitting room was full of residents and their families, and she smiled at several people she knew. Though she hadn't lived in Dennison for almost twenty years, she had come home often and stayed in touch with many of her childhood friends and their family members. It was comforting to return to her old church, see her former schoolteachers downtown, run into an old neighbor at the grocery store, and generally feel at home again. Cleveland had never felt so tight-knit or full of a sense of community. At least, not in the same way as her hometown.

Debbie stopped at the front desk with the record and phonograph. A volunteer sat there with a smile on his face.

"Good afternoon," he said. "I'm Steven. How can I help you?"

"Hi, Steven." Debbie returned his smile. "I'm looking for Raymond Zink."

"Ray?" Steven's grin widened. "He's holding court in the dining room this afternoon."

"Holding court?"

Steven shook his head as he chuckled. "You'll see. Dining room is that way and to the left." He pointed in the direction she should go.

"Thank you. Mind if I leave this phonograph here? It belongs to Mr. Zink, but it's a little heavy to haul around."

"Sure. I'll have someone take it to Ray's room for you, if you'd like."

"That would be great." She smiled as she walked down the hall, following the smell of pot roast and baked bread.

Even before she turned the corner into the dining room, she could hear Mr. Zink's voice. It was loud and clear, and he was telling the story of Old Bing, the service dog that had gone to war with the Gray brothers of Dennison in June of 1918.

Debbie stopped inside the doorway and listened as Mr. Zink continued his story. He sat in his wheelchair, near the upright piano, one of his hands resting on the ivory keys, as if he'd just finished playing a song. He was famous in Dennison for his piano playing.

Sitting around him were about a dozen people. Some looked like they were residents, while others appeared to be visiting family members. Mr. Zink held everyone's attention, from the youngest to the oldest.

"Bing was only nine days old when he was smuggled onto a troop ship by the Gray brothers, one hundred and five years ago this month," Mr. Zink said. "He went through basic training and served in active duty, with fifty-eight days in the trenches, and received two citations for bravery." Mr. Zink's body showed his advanced age, but his eyes lit up and his voice was strong as he spoke. "Old Bing survived being gassed twice and came back to Dennison with yellow teeth and patches of missing fur from the side effects. But for his service in the First World War, he received the regular sixty-eight-dollar bonus for discharged soldiers."

Debbie had heard the story of Old Bing before, but she never tired of it. When Mr. Zink saw her standing there, his face brightened with a smile and he excused himself from his audience to join her, pushing the wheels on his chair.

"Hello, Debbie. It's so nice to see you again."

"Hello, Mr. Zink." Debbie knew him from growing up in her church. When she decided to come back to Dennison to open the Whistle Stop Café, he heard she was looking for a house and offered his. It was almost miraculous how everything had fallen into place. "I'm happy to see you've found a new audience to share your passion for history."

"I won't stop until the Good Lord takes me home." He motioned to a chair. "First of all, everyone here calls me Ray. Second, have a seat and tell me why you're here. I hope everything is okay at the house."

"It's perfect. I love it." She set her bag down and pulled out the old record inside its sheath. "I actually came by to let you know there was a trunk left in the attic and I thought you might want it."

"A trunk?" Ray squinted. "What was in it?"

"Some newspapers, a portable phonograph, which is being delivered to your room, and this." She handed him the record.

Ray looked at it for a moment and then slowly slipped the record out of the sheath. His mouth began to quiver, and his gaze seemed to slip back in time. "My Eleanor." Finally, he looked at Debbie. "Where did you say you found this?"

"In an old trunk in the attic," she repeated, watching him closely. "I thought maybe you had forgotten it."

"I hadn't forgotten—how could I forget about her?" He held the record to his chest. "I haven't been able to get into that attic for almost a decade, and I was sure I'd lost this. I can't believe you found it."

"Who was she?" Debbie asked. "She had a beautiful singing voice."

"It was only a small part of her beauty." Tears filled Ray's eyes as he spoke. "I've never known a woman like Eleanor O'Reilly before or since."

"Was she your sweetheart?"

"She was more than that. She was my very heart and soul." He looked at the record again and tenderly ran his hand over the label. "She was supposed to be my wife."

"What happened to her?" Debbie asked.

He shook his head. "I don't know."

Debbie frowned. "You don't know?"

"When I left Dennison to join the army, she was standing on the platform at the depot to see me off. She promised to write and told me that when I returned, we'd be married." He swallowed and let out a sad sigh. "But her letters stopped abruptly, and when I came home, she wasn't here. I looked for her for months, but I never saw her again. I eventually came to the realization that she didn't love me. It was the only explanation I could come to." He was quiet for a moment, lost in his own thoughts. "I never loved again."

Debbie's heart broke for Ray. She had lost her fiancé when he died in Afghanistan as a special forces officer. It had been years, but sometimes it felt like yesterday. Would the pain remain with her as long as it had with Ray? The thought felt weighty and suffocating.

"Debbie?" Ray asked.

"Yes?"

"Would you help me find Eleanor? She probably doesn't want to hear from me, if she's still alive, but I've always wondered where she went and how she made out. It would do my heart good to know she was happy."

Debbie smiled. Though she had a house to remodel and a restaurant to open in less than three weeks, how could she say no to such a heartfelt request? "I'd love to help you."

His lips trembled, but his smile was radiant. "Can I tell you how I met Eleanor?" he asked.

Debbie couldn't wait to find out.

If you enjoyed this book, you might enjoy the
other books in this series!

MYSTERIES *of* MARTHA'S VINEYARD

A Light in the Darkness
Like a Fish Out of Water
Adrift
Maiden of the Mist
Making Waves
Don't Rock the Boat (also known as *Coast of Christmas Present)*
A Port in the Storm
Thicker Than Water
Swept Away
Bridge Over Troubled Waters
Smoke on the Water
Shifting Sands
Shark Bait
Seascape in Shadows
Storm Tide
Water Flows Uphill (also known as *Carol of the Ship's Bells)*
Catch of the Day
Beyond the Sea
Wider Than an Ocean
Sheeps Passing in the Night
Sail Away Home
Waves of Doubt
Lifeline
Flotsam & Jetsam
Just Over the Horizon

A NOTE FROM THE EDITORS

We hope you enjoyed another exciting volume in the Mysteries of Martha's Vineyard series, published by Guideposts. For over seventy-five years, Guideposts, a nonprofit organization, has been driven by a vision of a world filled with hope. We aspire to be the voice of a trusted friend, a friend who makes you feel more hopeful and connected.

By making a purchase from Guideposts, you join our community in touching millions of lives, inspiring them to believe that all things are possible through faith, hope, and prayer. Your continued support allows us to provide uplifting resources to those in need. Whether through our communities, websites, apps, or publications, we inspire our audiences, bring them together, and comfort, uplift, entertain, and guide them. Visit us at guideposts.org to learn more.

We would love to hear from you. Write us at Guideposts, P.O. Box 5815, Harlan, Iowa 51593 or call us at (800) 932-2145. Did you love *Carol of the Ship's Bells*? Leave a review for this product on guideposts.org/shop. Your feedback helps others in our community find relevant products.

Find inspiration, find faith, find Guideposts.

Shop our best sellers and favorites at

guideposts.org/shop

Or scan the QR code to go directly to our Shop

Find more inspiring stories in these best-loved Guideposts fiction series!

Mysteries of Lancaster County

Follow the Classen sisters as they unravel clues and uncover hidden secrets in Mysteries of Lancaster County. As you get to know these women and their friends, you'll see how God brings each of them together for a fresh start in life.

Secrets of Wayfarers Inn

Retired schoolteachers find themselves owners of an old warehouse-turned-inn that is filled with hidden passages, buried secrets, and stunning surprises that will set them on a course to puzzling mysteries from the Underground Railroad.

Tearoom Mysteries Series

Mix one stately Victorian home, a charming lakeside town in Maine, and two adventurous cousins with a passion for tea and hospitality. Add a large scoop of intriguing mystery, and sprinkle generously with faith, family, and friends, and you have the recipe for *Tearoom Mysteries.*

Ordinary Women of the Bible

Richly imagined stories—based on facts from the Bible—have all the plot twists and suspense of a great mystery, while bringing you fascinating insights on what it was like to be a woman living in the ancient world.

To learn more about these books, visit Guideposts.org/Shop